Dancing with Elephants

*Mindfulness Training
for Those Living with Dementia,
Chronic Illness, or an Aging Brain*

Jarem Sawatsky

RED CANOE PRESS / WINNIPEG

Red Canoe Press
266 Winnipeg
Winnipeg, Manitoba, R3G1X3, Canada
www.redcanoepress.com

Dancing with Elephants: Mindfulness Training for Those Living with Dementia, Chronic Illness or an Aging Brain / Jarem Sawatsky

How to Die Smiling Series 1

Publisher's Cataloging-In-Publication Data
(Prepared by The Donohue Group, Inc.)

Names: Sawatsky, Jarem.
Title: Dancing with elephants : mindfulness training for those living with dementia, chronic illness, or an aging brain / Jarem Sawatsky.
Description: Winnipeg, Manitoba, Canada : Red Canoe Press, [2017] | Series: How to die smiling series ; 1 | Based on the blog of the same name.
Identifiers: ISBN 9780995324206
Subjects: LCSH: Mindfulness (Psychology) | Sawatsky, Jarem--Mental health. | Aging--Psychological aspects. | Chronic diseases--Psychological aspects. | Peace of mind. | Self-actualization (Psychology) | Self-help techniques.
Classification: LCC BF637.M56 S29 2017 | DDC 158.1--dc23

ISBN 978-0-9953242-0-6

Get 5-Part Video Series FREE

You have *Dancing with Elephants*, Vol 1 in the How to Die Smiling Series.

Now get Vol 2 free.

A More Healing Way:
Video Conversations on Facing Disease

featuring Jon Kabat-Zinn, Patch Adams, Lucy Kalanithi,

John Paul Lederach and Toni Bernhard.

Hosted by Jarem Sawatsky ($200 value).

Details can be found at the end of *Dancing with Elephants*.

Reading Guide for *Dancing With Elephants* (great for individuals and book clubs) available at:

www.jaremsawatsky.com/dancing-guide

Reviews

...beautifully models a way to dance in the gale of full catastrophe, to celebrate life, to laugh with it and at himself...
- JON KABAT-ZINN, national bestselling author of *Full Catastrophe Living*

... a powerful example of the art of real happiness. This inspiring story reminds us just how essential it is to bring lovingkindness into every step of life, no matter how difficult the path.
-SHARON SALZBERG, New York Times bestselling author of *Real Happiness*

Life can be tough and it's even tougher without the ability to find humor. When life seems to be falling apart, Jarem Sawatsky's reminds us that laughter is what we need to not take ourselves too seriously.
-JEN MANN, New York Times bestselling author of *People I Want to Punch in the Throat*

... beautiful and inspiring... full of humor and wisdom about the pain of loss in our life,
-JEAN VANIER, national bestselling author of *Becoming Human*

CONTENTS

{ 1 }

Facing Elephants

D earest Elephant Dancer,

I know nothing about elephants nor dancing. And yet, this is a training manual and love letter for elephant dancers like yourself.

Facing elephants is something we often avoid. Most of us have elephants hidden in our closets, or hidden in plain sight. These elephants are our big, unacknowledged fears.

What are your elephants? What do you fear? Who gave you these elephants? How can you learn to love and dance with your elephants?

In this book, I serve as your guide in teaching the art of dancing with elephants. One of my big elephants is Huntington's disease—once called the dancing disease! It's an incurable, genetic, progressive, fatal brain disease. It is kind of a combination of Parkinson's, Alzheimer's and Schizophrenia. Just picture an elephant with this combo! That picture makes me laugh now. But I have not always been laughing.

I've never really known life without Huntington's disease lurking somewhere in the corner. Huntington's is genetic and so is passed down from generation to generation. It is a slow train wreck of a disease, sometimes lasting up to 25 years from first symptoms to death. In the olden days people would say, "Stay away from those families—they go crazy as they age and it is not pretty." When I was a child, my grandmother's generation had Huntington's, as did some of our more distant relatives. Several of them were put in asylums because not much was known about the disease. I was told to not worry because a cure would surely be found by the time I developed it, if I ever did. When I was in my teens, it was mom's generation's turn–my mother had it, as did all her siblings except for two brothers, one of whom was adopted. Huntington's seemed like a massive earthquake that left mostly rubble behind. As a teen, I was part of that rubble. When I started university, I began to focus on conflict and peace studies. I was interested in finding more healing ways to deal with injustice, harm, fear, and violence. By grace, I fell in love with Rhona Hildebrand, an elementary school music teacher. Before we were married, we had to have some careful discussions about Huntington's disease—yes, you can meet my mom but she is not well and can be quite explosive. No, I guess she doesn't treat me like a son... I told Rhona she should consider seriously whether she wanted to marry into a Huntington's disease family. I nervously awaited her response. In hindsight, I learned I had two things working in my favour: 1) She was raised by people who modeled loving through life's ups and downs and 2) I am a very good kisser and Rhona was hooked. So we got married. Rhona said we needed to include "in sickness and in health" in our vows. And so we did. After a couple of years of marriage, we moved to Virginia for a year so that I could earn a master's degree in conflict transformation. During that year, we got pregnant with identical twin girls. We moved back to Canada, where our wonderful daughters, Sara and Koila, were born. I taught conflict studies at two universities in Winnipeg. Teaching turned out to be a great fit, but I knew that if I wanted to continue to teach at the university level, I would need to get my doctorate. So I applied and got a full scholarship to the University of Hull in England. We moved there when the girls were three. It was in England that I started my research into communities that practiced healing justice. I traveled around the world, visiting Thich Nhat Hanh's Buddhist community in France; Hollow Water, an Indigenous community in Canada; and the Iona Community, a Christian community based in Scotland. These places are living examples of community life where injustices are addressed with healing and love rather than punishment, judgment, and fear. During this time, my mom died from Huntington's disease at the age of fifty-eight. We had to fly back from England for her final days and the funeral. Two years later, I completed my studies and was re-hired as Assistant Professor at Canadian Mennonite University. I published two books—one about research into restorative justice and peace-building that I had written in Virginia and the other about the three communities of healing justice that I had studied in England. My career as a teacher, researcher, and author was going very well. I got a government grant to allow me to continue travelling the world searching for communities of healing justice. The girls were in school and Rhona was back at work half time. Life was good. But we knew that because my mom had Huntington's disease, I had a 50/50 chance of getting it. My mother's main coping mechanism was to deny that she even had the disease. This left too many elephants lurking in the corners. There was a DNA blood test I could take that would tell me if I had inherited the gene for the disease. My mom could have had the test done a decade sooner than she did. While denial may have provided her some comfort, it made it profoundly difficult for any of us to support her on the journey. I wanted to chart a different path. First, I applied for early promotion at work. Once I was approved, both me and my brother had the testing done. I was positive. He was not. I would develop the disease. My daughters now had a 50/50 chance of having the disease.

For me, the news was both shocking and not shocking at all. I had always felt like I would get the disease. That insight provoked me to enjoy life in the present. However, having a doctor tell you that you will get this disease is, of course, different than listening to your own inner voice. The genetic counsellor had to make sure I wasn't suicidal over the news. When she asked what we were going to do next, I said, "We will throw a Movers & Shakers party with friends to welcome the next part of our journey." She asked if I was kidding. You can read about the party in Chapter 5 – Celebrate Everything.

The same day we learned my diagnosis, we told our girls and went on a short family vacation to process it. The doctors could not give me a timeframe for the onset but I started to visit a neurologist every eight months for a checkup. Four years later, in 2014, I began having symptoms. When it was time to see the neurologist again, I put together a self-assessment, comparing myself to the previous year. Rhona added to the list and we shared it with the neurologist and the social worker from the Huntington Disease Society. Here are some highlights from that list.

Movement (body):

- stiff ankles
- progressively poor typing skills
- involuntary foot and toe movement
- finger movement
- elbow movement, lots of spilling

- decreased spatial awareness – knocking into things
- tingling sensation in the top of head
- painful sensitivity to loud noises
- ringing in my ears
- some swallowing problems
- night-time leg twitches
- more sick days from work than ever before

Cognitive (mind):

- difficulty moving to the next task at work
- inability to multitask
- very distractible, can't keep focus very long
- hard time deciding on priorities
- tend to get an idea in my head, then get fixed on it
- altered sense of time—it seems to move very slowly, and I am more impatient
- hard to remember to follow through on short, easy tasks
- overwhelmed by email, and don't open most of it
- harder time making decisions
- hard to sustain complex research exploration
- slowed mental functioning
- loss of ambition—hard to self-motivate or initiate
- hard time remembering short grocery list
- hard time remembering/accessing the word I am looking for
- tend to take on job assignments at work and then not get work done
- foggy brain

Psychiatric (emotional & relational)

- depression
- don't seem to feel fear in situations I used to feel fear (e.g. heights)
- hard to move out of anger
- tend to be easily irritable
- avoid social settings
- constantly feel like a failure at work
- increasingly tired in the evenings and likelier to stay home and not relate to others
- tend to care less about mistakes
- loss of spontaneity – prefer to know what is coming

Rhona and I met with the neurologist and a social worker. After a bunch of discussion, the neurologist told us that it was time for me to quit work. This was in early July. Again, we went straight on vacation—a road trip across Canada—lots of time to process our new path, again.

On the advice of friends, we added a golden lab puppy named Kobi to our family. Sara and Koila are 15 now. Kobi is two. And I am literally stumbling my way into learning about loving, letting go, and living in the present moment.

I understand the agony, pain, and struggle of having your world turned upside down by disease and aging. I have watched Huntington's move through three generations. I look into the eyes of my daughters with the full knowledge that there's a 50/50 chance that they too have

Huntington's, passed on by me. After they turn 18, they will need to wrestle with whether or not to get the DNA test done. It is possible this disease may take another generation, my girls.

This is hard for all of us. In many ways, I have had lots of advantages in life. I have made studying conflict and healing my life's work. I do not want agony to be the main story of my life. I think agony, on its own, is toxic. I do not want to pass agony, fear, or violence onto Sara, Koila, or Rhona. So I have been experimenting on myself to find a healing way to face disease.

I am two years into these experiments and explorations. I will share my results with you. To help you understand the way I am trying to live well with disease, I need to first share the stories and the wisdom of some of the people who have influenced me the most on this journey.

When you find out that you are dying from an incurable disease, a kind of clarity can emerge. It is the clarity to distinguish between what matters and what does not matter. Having four university degrees and having experienced three generations of a debilitating disease, I had a lot of sorting to do. This book chronicles what I see as important. It is my cheat sheet for facing disease and aging in a healing kind of way.

When I had to "retire" at age 41 from my work as a university professor, I had hundreds of books. I gave away almost all of them. I saved the handful I thought might be helpful for me in learning the art of dancing with elephants.

The author with the greatest number in my little library is Zen Buddhist Master Thich Nhat Hanh. While he is not quoted much this book, Thay—as his students call him—lies at the heart of it. Thay is responsible for bringing a revitalized Engaged Buddhism to the west. He was nominated for a Nobel Peace Prize by Martin Luther King Jr. I had the privilege of spending time at his community, Plum Village, as part of my research on healing justice. Thay is an author of more than one hundred books. I find his writing and speaking deeply valuable. It is inspiring but also very concrete and practical. I was deeply shaped by Thay's focus on practicing wisdom in everyday life and living that wisdom in a community. In this book, I try to maintain this focus: true wisdom, lived in the everyday, supported in a community. The summer I was at Plum Village with my family, Thay taught the five mindfulness trainings. Each of the five parts of this book reflects one of these trainings.

Each section also includes an interview with a leader in the field of finding more healing ways of living. The featured teachers include the following:

Jon Kabat-Zinn, is the author of 10 books on mindfulness, trauma and health. He is known for mindfulness based stress reduction (MBSR) trainings which more than 16,000 people have successfully completed. MBSR was designed to develop relaxation and calm self-awareness, a reliable foundation for facing the "full catastrophe" of stress, pain, and illness—indeed, of life itself. In Chapter 6 Jon Kabat-Zinn dares us to focus on living now, rather than being paralyzed by the life we cannot live.

Patch Adams, M.D. who was made famous by the hit movie starring Robin Williams. Patch has been working on building a model hospital, modelled as an ecovillage where doctors and patients live together and where the doctor and the janitor get paid the same salary. Patch estimates he has been present at more than 10,000 deathbeds. In my interview with him in chapter 11, he talks about dying well and living well.

Lucy Kalanithi wrote the bestselling book *When Breath Becomes Air* with her 36-year-old neurosurgeon husband, Paul, as he was dying of stage IV metastatic lung cancer. Lucy, who is also a medical doctor and professor, spoke with me about true love in the face of diseases like cancer.

John Paul Lederach is the author of more than 22 books on conflict transformation, peace-building, and healing. John Paul—my former professor—and I discuss how his professional life and his faith has helped and hindered him in supporting his wife, Wendy, who has Parkinson's disease.

Toni Bernhard was a law professor at the University of California-Davis for 22 years until some fibromyalgia-like illnesses forced her to retire. In chapter 29, Toni and I discuss the three books she has written since, including *How to Live Well with Chronic Pain and Illness.*

The rest of the book offers glimpses of my wrestling, laughing, and stumbling my way into healing. Not the kind of healing that takes away the disease but the kind of healing that awakens the heart to love. I call this dancing with elephants because dancing is a playful way of engaging that which we fear most. Those who know me well know that playfulness is a major practice for me, as is the intentional use of humor. Suffering is real and must be faced head-on. But suffering alone is not enough. On the other side of suffering can be joy—and also more suffering. We must learn to dance with both.

Our culture offers abundant advice on how to achieve financial and career success, but there are very few books on how to embrace the downward path of losing your mind. We have success tips for leaders, but almost no "success tips" for the billions of us facing disease, dementia, and aging. This book is for those billions. Together we will explore the art of dancing with elephants.

I invite you to join me in this dance.

Part I
Reverence for Life

{ 2 }

Embracing the Hard Things

On Avoiding the Hard Things

Do prayers ever piss you off? Sometimes they piss me off. In my teens and twenties, I was a wilderness guide, leading group canoe trips. Sometimes participants on these trips would pray that it wouldn't rain. Even in my teens, I knew this made no sense. Sometimes I would prod.

"Do you want the trees and animals to die? They need rain."

"No," they would say. "We just don't want it to rain on us."

"Oh, so you want it to rain on the other groups I take out this summer, but not your group?"

"No," they would say. "God can make it rain on the trees and animals but not the people."

I already realized as a teen that it requires substantial mental (and sometimes theological) gymnastics for people to be able to justify a view of the world in which uncomfortable or unpleasant things shouldn't happen.

On the Way We Ride the Wave

This fall, I returned to that same wilderness of Canadian Shield country. It felt like coming full circle. Crossing paths with my younger self, I was reminded of the wisdom I could receive only by listening to the heartbeat of the wild. The temptation to try and insulate oneself from the hard things remains both common and understandable, but I still don't want to run from the storm. I don't want to run from the hard things. Healing is not the absence of the storm. Healing is the way we ride.

Driving alone on the prairies after going to the funeral of a young man, and thinking about my own chronic illness and about rain, I wrote this poem:

Nobody Wants the Rain

Everybody wants green scenery
Nobody wants the rain
Everybody wants food on the table
Nobody wants the rain
Everybody wants the colourful rainbow
Nobody wants the rain
Everybody wants water in their bodies
Nobody wants the rain

I went to the prairie,
The Expander of Horizons
To ask about the rain
I stood on the edge of the world
And watched the rain coming all around
And the prairie proclaimed a vision
Each time the gift of rain was offered
the people ran in fear
Heart's fear perverts darkness into evil
Missing the gift of life hidden in the cloud
Let it rain down, let it rain down
Let it rain down on me

Everybody wants green scenery
Nobody wants the rain
Everybody wants food on the table
Nobody wants the rain
Everybody wants the colourful rainbow
Nobody wants the rain
Everybody wants water in their bodies
Nobody wants the rain

I went to the mountain
The Giver of Wisdom
To ask about the rain
I knelt on ancient rocks
Fifty billion years awake

and the rocks spoke to me
The rain shapes and molds us
and turns us into sand
These rain-shaped rocks
Feed the earth as their dust becomes soil
The mighty mountains are transformed
By but a tiny drop of rain
Let it rain down, let it rain down
Let it rain down on me

Everybody wants green scenery
Nobody wants the rain
Everybody wants food on the table
Nobody wants the rain
Everybody wants the colourful rainbow
Nobody wants the rain
Everybody wants water in their bodies
Nobody wants the rain

I went to the ocean
The Alpha and Omega
To ask about the rain
I sat on the ocean's edge
As but a tiny grain of sand
And the ocean questioned me
Where is my beginning and
where is my end?
Ocean's edge is hard to find

On shore? In sky? Inside my body?
The ocean's end is its own beginning
Let it rain down, let it rain down
Let it rain down on me

We cannot learn to revere life if we cannot wrap our hearts around the idea that suffering exists. The art of dancing with elephants is not the elimination of suffering. We don't kill the elephant. We learn to dance with it. All living beings suffer. To revere life, we cannot remain in denial but must understand that suffering and death are inevitable. This truth is not the end of the story but it is a necessary starting point on this journey.

Once we become comfortable with the idea that suffering exists, we need to learn to let go of fear and replace it with love. This is the focus of the next chapter.

{ 3 }

Replacing Fear with Love

The next step in learning to dance with elephants is to learn to overcome fear. Fear lies at the root of much unnecessary suffering. Overcoming fear will dissolve some kinds of suffering. The suffering that remains needs to be accompanied by love.

On October 27, 2010, I tested positive for the gene for Huntington's. This meant that I would get the disease that had killed my mother and a number of her relatives. Among other things, this disease is a long, slow degeneration to death. Through this disease, over the course of about twenty years, I get to practice the spiritual discipline of letting go of everything that I had thought made me human: eating, walking, sitting still, control of muscles, speaking.

Exactly one month after testing positive for the Huntington's gene, I was to preach in the small Christian church community where I grew up. I agonized about what to say. One of the practices that was giving me joy and freedom at that time came from a meditation that I had learned in Plum Village. Fresh with the perspective that I should speak out of my experience (rather than primarily out of my thinking), I modified a meditation on bones to use language that more of my Christian friends would understand. That Sunday, I told the community about my diagnosis. I told them that if there is an elephant in the room that won't go away (like Huntington's) at least we can learn to dance with it. And I taught them the practice that was helping me learn how to dance with the elephant. It is a practice of transforming fear into joyful dancing, called Corpse Prayer. It's not an easy practice but it does seem to bear good fruit in me and others. And so I offer this practice to you as a tool that may help you begin to dance with your own elephant.

Corpse Prayer

I want you to take a moment to imagine the last three minutes of your life. Where will you be? What will you be doing? Who else is there? Will it be sudden? Will you be suffering? Will you have suffered for a long time already? What emotions and thoughts will you be experiencing?

Imagine the scene as if you were watching it on a TV screen. Notice the emotions that arise within you as you watch. Do not identify yourself with these emotions, but recognize that they are rising within you. If these emotions are primarily fear and anxiety, then you know this is a tender topic that needs your careful attention. Let us practice loving yourself at the point of your death.

As you picture yourself dying, try saying these phrases:

Be not afraid.
I give thanks to God who created all things good.
In Christ, all things hold together.
I am not entitled to life without death.
I embrace sacred life. I embrace sacred death. I embrace
the growing and crumbling in between.

Smile at yourself in the silence...

Now picture the moment your body is being buried. Think of that moment when your body returns to the earth, when your coffin is lowered and reaches the end of its journey.

Picture yourself there. See the movie. Notice the emotions that arise within you. Do not identify yourself with these emotions but recognize that they are rising within you.

As you picture yourself dead and just starting to decay, try saying these phrases:

Be not afraid.
I give thanks to God who created all things good.
In Christ all things hold together.
I am not entitled to life without death.
I embrace sacred life. I embrace sacred death. I embrace
the growing and crumbling in between.

Smile at yourself…

Now picture your body two years after your death, when your body is decomposing and the worms are eating your flesh.

As you picture yourself dead and well decayed, try saying these phrases:

Be not afraid.
I give thanks to God who created all things good.
In Christ all things hold together.
I am not entitled to life without death.
I embrace sacred life. I embrace sacred death. I embrace
the growing and crumbling in between.

Smile at yourself in the silence…

Now picture your body eighty years later, when all that is left is bone, or move even further into the future and watch as even your bones turn to dust. Attend to your emotions.

As you picture yourself dead and turning to dust, try saying these phrases:

Be not afraid
I give thanks to God who created all things good

In Christ all things hold together.
I am not entitled to life without death.
I embrace sacred life. I embrace sacred death. I embrace
the growing and crumbling in between.

Smile at yourself in the silence…

For me this practice is freeing, even humourous. If in the end all is dust, I can let go of some of my fear, anxiety, and self-absorption. If in the end all is dust, then now is the time to enjoy, to play, to love. The fruits of this kind of freedom are countless.

Transforming Road Rage

Of course, life is still full of struggles. But replacing fear with love helps us as we face them. Let me give just one taste of the fruits of living with less fear.

One day last year, I was driving our car in downtown Winnipeg, heading out with my wife, Rhona, on a lunch date. From behind us, we could hear a horn blaring. Some seconds later, I stopped for a red light and saw a young man in a large, shiny truck with extended suspension in the next lane. I looked up at him. He was yelling and glaring at me. In the past, I probably would have been afraid and would have suppressed my fear until it came out later, directed at some other target. But this time, things unfolded differently. I glared back at him. As he struck different poses, I copied them. I saw his passenger window was open, so I rolled down my driver's side window. I think I wanted to hear what he was saying. But before I made any plan or intentional decision, I found myself calling out to him, *"Parlez-vous Francais?"* politely asking if he speaks French! On my right, I saw my wife instinctively pretending to be a deaf person reading an imaginary book. On the other side of me was the young man in the big truck, full of rage. After an awkward silence, he said "No," and gave a big sigh. He de-escalated and backed right down and so did I. Who knew the language of love (French, I mean) had the power to transform fear and road rage into humour. After my wife's disappearing act ended, her fear turned to laughter. "Did you just pretend to speak only French?" she asked. "Yes," I answered, though in truth I speak very little French at all.

I know this was probably not the most honest or most loving response. But responding with playfulness rather than fear transformed the situation. When you let go of fear, a new vista starts to emerge. This new vista is a meadow, with plenty of room to explore, to play, to laugh, and to love. Perhaps the Corpse Prayer can help free you. Or if that doesn't work, try laughing.

There is much healing we can do when fear is replaced by love. Fear makes us defend life, like some possession, at all costs. Love provides a way to revere life without treating it as a possession. Great elephant dancers need to start learning anew to revere life. To help us hold sacred life as it is, we need to learn the art of seeing.

{ 4 }

Letting Go

It is only when we lose something or have it taken from us, that we realize we feel entitled to it. Then we have to wrestle with what life means without our entitlements. Anyone who has dementia, chronic illness, or an aging brain knows what this feels like.

This poem, "Letting Go," represents some of the questions I have been asking myself. I wrote this while still working and anticipating that I would need to go on long-term disability.

Letting Go

How deeply can I let go of entitlement?
Can I let go of entitlement to work?
To status
To being productive
To right livelihood
To gainful employment
To forms of vocation

Can I let go of the entitlement to body control?
To controlling movement of limbs
To controlling bladder and bowel
To looking "normal"
To eating quietly and cleanly
To a voice that is respected
Can I let go of entitlement to emotional stability?
To controlling anger
To a predictable response
To understanding my own responses
Can I let go of the entitlement to self-reliant
transportation?
To drive a car
To ride a bike
To walk long distances
Can I let go of the entitlement to be accepted by others?
To smiles from strangers
To lovemaking with my lover
To gratefulness of students
To being asked for help
Can I let go of entitlement to time?
To a future
To grandchildren
To being at a child's wedding
To memory
Some entitlements are harder to give up than others
Yet it is not our entitlements that make us human
But rather Creator's gift of a still fragile life

On the other side of entitlement lies more joy than
sorrow
How do I get to the other side?

Perhaps poetry can be part of the art of dancing with elephants. Thich Nhat Hanh has always encouraged his students to write poems. When you write a poem, the poem lives in you.

So I dare you to write poetry. If you are not poetic, take me as your guide and write bad poetry. It does not matter if you think of your poetry as bad or good but rather that it comes from the heart and that it helps you walk in a healing way.

Ask yourself: "What do I need to let go of in order to embrace life in the here and now?"

Write a poem to teach yourself to let go of entitlements.

Then sing it in the shower. Chant it as you walk. Say your words through the tears, the fears, and even through the laughter.

I have one more dare for you. Share your poetry on letting go. Let go of your fear of what others may think of your poetry. Share it with your circle of friends and consider sharing it on my Elephant Dancers Facebook Group. As we practice our poetry and the art of letting go, we can be nourished by one another's insights. So go to this page: www.jaremsawatsky.com/facebook. Let me know which email to send your group invitation to and I will send it to you. Then you can post poems and reflections for other elephant dancers to see. Let go. I dare you.

{ 5 }

Celebrating Everything

A Celebration for Losing Your Mind

W estern culture is better at celebrating beginnings than endings. We know what to do with births and marriages but don't do as well with deaths or divorces. We know even less about celebrating what we see as disability.

When I was told I had the gene for Huntington's and that I would get the disease, the genetic counselor asked what I planned to do. I said we would throw a big party. She thought I was joking at first. But I wasn't. My Huntington's diagnosis brought immense changes to my life and my family and we needed to mark this transition. We needed to eat and laugh together, to remember and celebrate as a community.

Huntington's disease, which causes constant uncontrolled movements, used to be known as a dancing disease. So we decided that this party should be a Movers & Shakers party. Originally, I wanted to invite everyone to bring a drink or food to share that shakes—martini, jello, milkshakes. In the end we let this piece go, but we did eat together—homemade wood-fire pizza, drinks, and lots of desserts.

If you look at almost any culture, you can see that healing and peacemaking steps are often steeped in the practice of eating together. In most cultures around the world, it would be unthinkable to try to make peace without the practice of feasting together. Sharing the very things that make for life—like food—is a sacred way to be together. For me, it was a profound time of communion.

Knowing that memory loss is a part of Huntington's disease, we were encouraged to start creating memory books—pictures and stories of where we've been. In the long-run, these would be invaluable. So as part of our party, we set out to create a book—of pictures of the party, but also of stories, emails, and memories of friends and family. We asked a professional photographer (focphotography.com) to come record the event. She took the job but refused payment! People from around the world, as well as friends at home, shared memories of me. It was as if they were holding up a mirror, reflecting back to me who I have been. What a gift!

We are surrounded by many great friends. Hearing our news was traumatic for them. Many wanted to help but didn't know how. At this event, some of our friends reminded us that we needed to be teachers for them in how to walk this path together. People wanted to help but needed to be shown how they could be supportive. So we organized our Movers & Shakers party and invited our various circles of friends and colleagues to celebrate "my retirement" in a way that made sense to us. We needed to mark this event, which was both an ending and a beginning, with the same conviction we had marked previous life events. Had someone else planned the party, it might not have felt right for Rhona and me. We put together an epic event, a party that was a profound and healing celebration to help us and our community mark my transition to living with Huntington's disease.

We didn't set out to create sacred time. But after the party, a person who had been to the party spoke about how profound the experience was and how incredible it felt to share that party with our family and our circles of friends. In some ways this was an awkward event. We didn't have a model to follow. Would this be a time of mourning or celebration or boring speeches? It turned out that our Movers & Shakers party was a time of compassion—which literally means "to suffer together"—and celebration. I highly recommend it to anyone!

For elephant dancers, celebration is a mindfulness training. Celebrate everything. We do not know what will happen tomorrow but we can find an excuse to celebrate today.

{ 6 }

Living the Life You've Got with Jon Kabat-Zinn

From our perspective, no matter what diagnosis you come with or what's wrong with you, there is more right with you than wrong with you—no matter what is 'wrong with you.'

It was like someone just smacked me on the head and I fell awake. More right with me than wrong with me? The man speaking knows I have Huntington's disease. In fact, he has spent his whole career working with people who have chronic and terminal diagnoses. At his own Stress Reduction Clinic, he has helped thousands of people who are facing profound suffering.

He kept saying it throughout our conversation: "If you are not dead yet—people, as long as you are breathing, from our perspective (big smile) there is more right with you than is wrong with you, no matter what is wrong with you."

Living on long-term disability with a chronic and terminal condition, I have a huge list of specialists I can call on to help with what is wrong with me: neurologist for brain problems, psychiatrist for problems in the psyche, speech and language pathologist for speaking problems, dietitian for food problems. The medical literature on my condition divides it into stages based on the inability to do things. More negative, problem-based thinking! I need to be careful not to see myself as one huge, fragmented problem. Although the experts call themselves health professionals, it seems to me that they are forced to act as disease or problem specialists.

But Jon Kabat-Zinn was pointing toward a different, more freeing way.

Feed What Is Working Rather than What Is Not

Jon founded Mindfulness-Based Stress Reduction (MBSR), an eight-week program that is used in hundreds of hospitals around the world. His books have sold millions of copies because he is onto something. During our conversation, he explained to me the purpose of MBSR.

> *We are going to let the rest of medical and health care system take care of what is 'wrong with you' and instead we will pour energy into*

*what is right with you, in the form of affection-
ate and kind attention—and we see what
happens. What happens is, people are tremendously energized by that invitation.*

Jon is clear that there is a role for western medicine
but he is also aware that the health care system sometimes contributes to unhealth and that those with
profoundly difficult, long-term conditions often fall between the cracks and gaps.

Jon's work is to dare people to live better lives, even
if no cure is possible. While he draws on Buddhist approaches, he is not a Buddhist. Mindfulness, he told me,
is a way to live life: "The more you cultivate this pre-
sent-moment, non-reactive, non-judgmental, open-
hearted presence—or attention or awareness—the more
it can become your default mode."

When I am told there is no cure for my condition, it is
easy to focus on "Why not?" or "Poor me" or "I don't
want to die." That reaction adds suffering to suffering. I
sought out Jon because I knew he could teach me about
living well to the end. He told me, "We all have a terminal condition, called living. The question is, are you still
living?"

There Is a Way to Hold Your Suffering and Be at Home in Your Body

*The basic message is a very hopeful one. There
is a way to hold all of your story—the full ca-*

tastrophe—that is not only integrating and joy-
ful, in a certain way, but that also gives your
life back to you in ways that are very hopeful
and optimistic.

Jon knows his task is to liberate people. In working with people with chronic and terminal conditions, he first focuses on freeing them from their own stories and from the stories they've absorbed from others, stories which suck the life right out of them. His approach is rooted in wisdom gleaned from witnessing thousands of people who have been in this spot and who have figured out how to get their lives back. This is hopeful. It is the hope of knowing that what you need is right here; it's not the hope of escaping from this place. I like this hope.

During our conversation, he challenged me: "Yes, maybe you have deficits or losses and they may get worse in the future, but how you are in relation to them in this moment can make an enormous difference in coping with the things that cannot be changed. We know enough about science to realize that your thoughts, emotions, and the stories you tell yourself about the future—about how inadequate you are, or how hopeless things are, or whatever— all that affect your very biology. You need to learn to be at home in your body, mind, and heart."

I commented, "Those people who are at home with themselves cause a lot less suffering to those around them and those trying to help them. The ripples keep on going."

"Yes, that is right," he said, getting excited. "This is not just a nice little stress reduction for myself to lead a happier, healthier life. When you do this kind of interior work, the social effects are profound: not just in your family (although they benefit) and not just in your workplace, but throughout the world, because of the ways in which the entire universe is interconnected."

Reclaiming the Present Moment

For Jon, the key to living in a healing way is to reclaim the present moment. Listen to some of his insights:

While you are still breathing, no matter how long you have to live—and that is an unknown— can you reclaim the present moment? That is tremendously healing, even in profoundly difficult situations.

We are all finite beings. We are all going to die. But the real question is, before we die, can we live fully? The dying usually takes care of itself. It is the living that is the real challenge.

Am I living the life I am supposed to be living or am I living a caricature of that life? Am I so distracted and caught up in getting someplace else that I am missing the preciousness and the uniqueness of moments on the way to wherever it is I think I need to go to be happy?

As one with a chronic condition, I need to be careful not to get caught in the past—in yearning for the life I had. I also need to be careful not to get caught up in the future—mourning the life I will not have. Both the past and the future can be toxic for us. When we let go of trying to get someplace else, we fully live each moment. Once we start being nourished by the present, our craving for the life we cannot have diminishes.

Losing Your Senses Without Losing Who You Really Are

"Even if you pour energy into what is right with you and you are compassionate with yourself, you will still lose yourself over time," Jon said. "As we age, we are all losing our senses, biologically. But we are not losing who we really are."

I know these are not flippant words. Jon's father had dementia for ten years. He offered more advice. "In terms of the progression of cognitive deficits, or losing our senses—hearing, touch, taste, or whatever, or balanced walking—those losses can be folded into the meditation practice," he said. "Instead of the greatest scourge, they can become the greatest teacher of all."

This is one of the great gifts of mindfulness. You can use the very thing you fear as a tool to replace fear with love. I know he was offering me powerful medicine.

From the time I was 16 years old, I have meditated looking at my steady hands, knowing that someday they might not be steady because of Huntington's. Each time, I meditated until I was OK with this possibility. Meditating on my hands has freed me from the expectation that my life should not include having Huntington's disease. It has taught me not to get caught up in hoping for a future that may be impossible for me. It has taught me to hold my career lightly and to not over-identify with it, as it could easily end. There is a mountain of suffering that I have not had to tunnel through because I lucked into a meditation practice in my teens.

Jon was trying to save me from suffering over things that do not require suffering. This was an act of love.

Mindfulness as a Radical Act of Love

As our discussion neared its end, Jon looked at me and tried to offer a raft of compassion for the journey ahead. He wanted to make sure I was getting the heart and spirit of his message. "When all is said and done, all that mindfulness is, is a radical act of love," he said. "To drop in on yourself in the present moment and to string some of these moments together in open-hearted presence. It is a radical act of sanity and reclaiming your humanity in the only moment any of us ever have. And that changes everything!"

If, in the end, it comes down to living in love, I think I can do that. Even with holes in my brain, I can love. Even with no cure, I can love. Do I need speech for love? Do I really need to hold my body still to be able to love? There are a lot of things I need to let go of, and I have tried to work on those, but if what's in the center is love, to me that is a liberating idea that connects me with everyone.

Jon knows choosing to face reality and to live in a healing way is not easy. "This is a deep existential choice, which is itself a radical act of love," he said. "Choosing not to fall into despair when that is a kind of default mode is hard. Some people don't make this choice. And yet this is something every single person is capable of doing. It is not like you need to go to college or be a university professor, or anything like that. Any single person is capable of doing the work of waking up, if they have the appropriate support and motivation. It means living our lives as if they really matter, and they do."

This kind of compassion or mindfulness is not about learning the right ideas or concepts. It is about practicing compassion daily, on a lifelong basis. Whatever senses we have available to us—hearing, vision, touch, smell, and taste—we can use them to wake up to non-reactive, non-judgmental, open-hearted presence—to love. All of Jon's books offer very specific ways to awaken the heart of compassion.

I recorded our interview as part of a five-part series, "A More Healing Way: Video Conversations on Disease." In the full video conversation, we explore other themes as they relate to mindfulness, such as global warming, President Trump, indigenous traditions, and full-catastrophe living. You can also hear Jon recite two of his favorite poems. To get a free copy of the video series, sign up for my Readers Group and I will send it your way.

(www.jaremsawatsky.com/more-healing)

Part II
True Happiness

{ 7 }

Living Beauty Awake

When my dear friend Kathy Barkman died, her husband, Lyle, asked me to offer a teaching at her funeral. This section, with some minor alterations, is the teaching I gave at her funeral on March 29, 2016. Kathy died from cancer at age 57. She had also lived with Multiple Sclerosis for many years. Kathy was a person of deep joy and happiness through all the ups and downs of life. She is a great example of true happiness.

When Lyle asked me to offer a teaching, he said there was a new song by Steve Bell, a Juno-Award winning artist (and friend) that totally captured the essence of Kathy's stunning, simple beauty. He sent me the lyrics and a demo of the song. You can hear "Let Beauty Awake" by going to this website:

https://soundcloud.com/steve_bell/let-beauty-awake.

I listened to the song while contemplating the life and death of our dear sister and friend from my own perspective, as someone with Huntington's disease, trying to live well in the face of certain death. After listening repeatedly, I decided that I would use the unfolding of the song to try to articulate what I saw as the gift and challenge of Kathy's life and death.

I offer four lessons of how Kathy lived beauty awake.

The Art of Beholding the Sacred

To me, the first verse of the song is about the art of beholding the sacred or, to put it another way, the art of attention. Listen:

Let beauty awake in the morn from beautiful dreams,
Beauty awake from rest!
Let Beauty awake
For Beauty's sake
In the hour when the birds awake in the brake
And the stars are yet bright in the west!
Let beauty awake from rest

The poet starts with everyday experiences that all of us share—morning, sunrise, dreams, rest. And he dares us to clothe everyday activities in beauty awake. Anyone who has sat quietly watching the sun's first kiss of the earth in the early morning knows the beauty of which the song speaks. And yet the song invites us to move beyond the spectacular one-off, awe-filled moment. Because beyond the spectacular lies the beauty of the mundane; that is beauty in everyday life. It is seeing and responding to beauty in every moment of the day, or at least as often as we can. I see this as the art of beholding the sacred.

Kathy was a genius at beholding others! She saw deep into you, her eyes touching your sacred beauty and goodness. Kathy had a bold, quiet attentiveness. Anyone who got close to Kathy—no matter their age or social status, could feel the warm attentiveness of her gaze. Kathy knew her attention was like a watering can—whatever she gave her attention to would grow. She gave her attention to others.

I think Kathy lived a beauty awake life because she recognized and beheld the beauty of others. Elizabeth Barrett Browning said, "Earth's crammed with heaven / And every common bush afire with God; / But only he who sees, takes off his shoes" (from Aurora Leigh).

This was Kathy—she was a shoe-taking-off kind of woman. She was one who truly saw deeply, beholding the sacredness of the everyday. Kathy knew and practiced the art of beholding.

The Art of Dynamic Loving

In the second verse of the song, it is as if the poet starts again with the beauty of the common and the art of beholding, but then suggests that the art of beholding is not enough. If you want to follow the enfolding path of beauty awake, you need to go deeper. Seeing the sacred is not enough, you need to add the dynamic to and fro of the art of love. Listen:

Let Beauty awake in the eve from the slumber of day,
Awake in the crimson eve!
In the day's dusk end
When the shades ascend,
Let her wake to the kiss of a tender friend
To render again and receive!
Let beauty awake in the eve

Anyone who has been married for at least a year, knows that the dynamic giving and receiving of love is a messy business—where we are sometimes meeting each other and sometimes missing each other. This kind of dynamic love, which the poet calls rending and receiving, is always changing. If we want to live beauty awake, we have to learn the art of loving in the midst of ongoing change. This is no easy task. The art of dynamic love is about constantly learning to love anew.

Kathy knew about the art of dynamic love. She and Lyle were married far longer than a year—their journey together was a beautiful, messy journey of soulmates unleashed. Kathy knew more than her share of suffering and health issues. Consequently, she knew more than her share of prayer.

If Kathy were a song-writer, I think she could have written these words Leonard Cohen wrote at a time of grave illness:

If it be your will
That a voice be true
From this broken hill
I will sing to you
From this broken hill
All your praises they shall ring
If it be your will to let me sing.

Kathy did sing beautifully from her broken hill. As the world kept changing, she kept finding new ways to love those of us who had the huge gift of living alongside this dear woman.

The Art of Gardening Creation Blessed

To me, each new section of the song starts with a kind of implied critique. It is as if the poet is saying, *you like the art of beholding and the art of dynamic loving, well it is not enough.* If you want to live beauty awake, you have to go deeper. It is not enough to see deeply and love deeply.

The poet warns we cannot be bystanders of the sacred, only watching it and loving it. Rather the poet calls us to engage the world in the here and now. To touch the earth as creation blessed. To touch the earth and the world as sacred and holy, and then to transform this sacred soil into the beauty of the flower. Listen:

> *While we, the gardeners of creation blessed*
> *Furrow the soil at our saviour's behest*
> *And bury the seeds of our own life's death*
> *And suffer God's glory to grow*

Kathy was not a bystander of the sacred. Kathy was a gardener of the sacred. Where others sought the spotlight, Kathy loved as any had need. From the youngest to the oldest, Kathy loved all.

I've come to see the Parable of the Sower from scriptures (Matt 13:3-9) as a story about a wasteful gardener who keeps throwing seed where there is a very slim chance of success. What kind of gardener throws seed on the path, or rocky ground, or among the thorns?

Kathy was like this so-called wasteful gardener—planting seeds in love was more important than succeeding. Part of the way Kathy lived beauty awake was to seek out those who were suffering and simply be a loving presence in their midst. There were other ways Kathy was a gardener of the sacred: She helped plant and cultivate a bakery rooted in love and justice. (Tall Grass Prairie Bread Company is a local, organic bakery that pays its farmers and staff higher than average rates. Kathy helped start and sustain this bakery. Incidentally, my twin girls both work there). While Kathy was not a proud person, I think one of her favourite acts of gardening creation was helping to raise sons into men of love.

Now, these are very advanced sacred gardening tech-
niques—but Kathy was in love with her family. Ben and
Dan, you are the living embodiment of your mother's art
of sacred gardening.

Let Beauty Awake from Death

In this last verse, it seems to me that the poet tries to
trick us. Having sucked us in with the beauty of sunrise
and sunset, having taught us the art of beholding, the art
of dynamic loving, the art of gardening creation blessed,
the poet unveils the centre, the gift hidden in this journey. It's as if we have climbed the mountain and now get
to see from the summit the secret of life. The big reveal:
Let Beauty Awake from Death. Listen:

Let Beauty awake, in the morn from the cool of the
grave,
Beauty awake from death;
Let Beauty awake,
For Jesus' sake,
In the hour when the angels their silence break
And the garden is bright with His Breath.
Let beauty awake from death

Lyle, Ben, and Dan, this is the chapter of Kathy that
we are all still writing. Kathy lived her life as a profound
example of Beauty Awake. But now, what of her death?

Listening to the song over and over, I started to fight with the poet.

Is death not the interruption of beauty awake? Isn't death the robber of beauty awake? Did we not pray that God would save Kathy and us from this day? Now, here in the presence of Kathy's dead body, among mourning friends and family, here you want me to say let beauty awake from death? Really? At first I was jealous of the songwriter. He ends his song, "Let beauty awake from death," but offers few clues as to what that means. How are we to hear those words today? The song offers nothing. "Let beauty awake from death," La, la, la, hum, hum. Sudden end. Thanks, Steve.

As I kept listening to the song, it was as if the poet whispered in my ear.

Did you not know this journey leads to death?

Did you not know that to live beauty awake you must also embrace beauty in death?

Then it was as if the poet whispered into my ear, almost mocking: *If you did not know this journey includes beauty from death, then go back to the beginning and see again with eyes of beauty awakening from death.*

Did I not point you to the sunrise and sunset?

Did I not give you this mini birth and death of sun everyday on the large screen of sky?

And did I not make both the birth and death of the sun beautiful? Did I not give you the beautiful birthing and beautiful dying of the sun so that every day you could practice embracing the beauty of life and the beauty of death?

Did I not make you gardeners of this sacred soil so that every time you put your hands on this messy, dark soil, you could practice touching death and know that it is OK?

Did I not tell you to touch the soil of creation blessed, so that you would learn what every gardener knows to be true: there is no beauty of life without also the death of life—together created very good?

And so the chapter we are still writing about Kathy is about beauty from death. The challenge I think we are left with is, how can Kathy's way of living beauty awake provide us with guidance in embracing her dying in beauty awake? How do we take all the insights of her life and apply them to her death?

Tomorrow, as her body is laid back into the ground, she gets to return to this soil we call creation blessed. Often, as the body is laid to rest, someone speaks the words from Genesis: Ashes to ashes, dust to dust. Remember, these words are not a curse. They are a blessing and a dare to the living. You were created from the earth and to the earth you are intended to return. You were created from dust and to dust you shall return. Ashes to ashes, dust to dust. These words beg us to live our lives embracing our dustness, not as a curse but as a blessing of beauty awake. So that from the cool of the grave of our dear friend and sister, we can say with deep loving kindness: Let beauty awake from death.

Song Credits
"Let Beauty Awake"
Music by Steve Bell
Lyrics for stanzas one and two: Robert Louis Stevenson
Stanzas three and four: Steve Bell
Stanza five: Tom Wright

{ 8 }

Embracing Dustness

It's a kind of deep anxiety rooted in the fear of disappointing others.

I was speaking to Rhona while taking our puppy, Kobi, on a walk through our neighbourhood. I was trying to communicate why walking the dog in our neighborhood had become stressful and anxiety-producing for me. Stress is not new to me but this kind of anxiety is new. When I walk the dog, I try to plot a path though our neighbourhood so that I will not run into anyone I know. This is quite difficult—and almost funny—as I have lived in the neighbourhood since I was eight years old! As I reflected on this anxiety, I realized it was not rooted in a fear of having to talk about Huntington's disease. I do that quite openly. Rather, it is a fear of letting others down. Growing up, I was a people-pleaser and overachiever. As Huntington's disease progresses, I am less able to please or achieve. My internal voice says, "Watch out. You will only disappoint them."

I know I have great friends, and so this is not about them. It is entirely about the perceptions in my head.

As I was complaining to Rhona about how I let this social anxiety create a maze of barricades, we were interrupted. A man on the other side of the street was yelling and waving. I had never seen this man. But Rhona and I became completely silent. We both knew. From across the street, in a manner of seconds, we had both diagnosed this man with advanced stages of Huntington's. He was doing the Huntington's dance. (If you want to get a sense of what this looks like, check out this two-minute video and song, which I found online. It is called the Huntington's Dance:

https://www.youtube.com/watch?v=e50WiWgIbxg.)

The man we saw was largely non-verbal, could barely stand up, and was waving at us. His dog sat still beside him. As people passed by him on the other side of the street, we noticed he was welcoming everyone he met as a friend! We went and talked to him and confirmed our diagnosis and learned his name was Rob. We told him I also have the disease. There was a deep kindness in him.

Later that night, Rhona asked me, "So what did you think of seeing Rob today?"

"I was complaining of social anxiety and he was welcoming everyone he met. Ironic," I replied. I thought to myself that this man needs to be my teacher. He knew about compassion, freedom, embracing strangers, overcoming anxiety, and loving the world.

I reflected on the kind of wisdom that was present in Rob's way of being and I wondered how I could get past my anxiety to share in that wisdom. I was reminded of an exercise I had done with my university students in a class on non-violence, that I thought might help me in this task. In the non-violence class, we explored Gandhi's way of being and his statement that "the seeker after truth should be humbler than dust." To help my students become friends with that kind of imagination, I made them all write poems to try to unlock the wisdom of this statement. Realizing that writing poems requires a kind of willingness to be vulnerable, I decided that I should write my own poem. It reflects the spirit in which I wish to walk the path ahead, the way in which I hope to learn to be like Rob.

Embracing Dustness

Dust to dust
Ashes to ashes
This is no curse
Or last words of lament
It is a riddle key
To the way of Truth
It's a riddle key
To a life of nonviolence
The lover of truth
Embraces the way of the dust
The dust is free
Free from all striving

-to be on top
-to maintain control
-to become bigger and better
The dust does not consent
To the rules of the powerful
This non-consenting dustness
Transforms, even enemies
From below
it looks down on none
and can be crushed by any
And the one who can be crushed by any
Has defeated defeat
Winning and losing collapse
The dust-filled lover is hindered by neither
Humbler than dust
is the way of Truth
The lovers of truth embrace
the way of the dust

To many, embracing dust does not sound like true happiness. I think that to understand the true happiness that comes from this practice, you must give it a try. My experience is that embracing dust can teach us a lot about dancing with elephants and about true happiness.

There is a Swahili proverb, "When two elephants fight, it is the grass that suffers." The proverb communicates a kind powerlessness that the grass feels when both dominated and ignored by larger powers. But think of the dust. The dust does not suffer in the same way as the grass. The dust is an image of resilience that transcends power and powerlessness.

If we are going to dance with elephants, we will get dirty. If we see the dirt as a curse, we will never be happy. If we see dirt as the way of dustness, then we can dance with elephants and get dirty; we can still be people who are truly happy.

{ 9 }

Walking the Urban Pilgrimage

Walking is a long-used mindfulness practice for those interested in a more healing and peaceful way. Mahatma Gandhi, Martin Luther King Jr, and Thich Nhat Hanh are well known for using walking in the service of building peace. However, they walked very differently from one another. It is a good thing they did not walk together! Gandhi would have won any race—he walked with speed, determination, and an inward, almost introverted focus. Martin Luther King Jr. would be second in a race. King walked as an extrovert, engaging others with a slow, pounding pace like a drum. Thich Nhat Hanh would be last in any walking race. With the speed of a tortoise, he would slowly take each step, as if it was his first and his last step to ever touch holy land.

Many spiritual traditions have some form of walking pilgrimage as a way to awaken the heart and soul and to honor the sacred. For many in my circle of friends and acquaintances, *The Camino de Santiago* in Spain is the ultimate holy walking experience.

When I first went on long-term disability, I started walking. I had these voices of Gandhi and King and an image of sacred pilgrimage in mind. I also had in mind the voice of a Buddhist nun whom I had met during a visit to Plum Village—Thich Nhat Hanh's community. I asked what she thought was the most important mindfulness practice for non-Buddhists. To my surprise, she responded immediately: "Walking Meditation." So with these various voices in mind, I walked. Sometimes, these voices would fight with one another about the more sacred way to walk. But they found common cause when questions of *where* to walk arose.

Why do we need to go to the other side of the world to find sacred spaces? Such travel is the luxury of the rich and often the able-bodied. If we cannot touch and respond to the sacred in each step at home, what makes us think we will do better in some other place? If we do better in some other place, will it really help us walk each step, mindful of the sacred, when we return?

These questions led me to dare myself: Walk a sacred pilgrimage at home. Gandhi's famous Salt March was 386 km (240 miles) in 23 days—about 17 km a day. From having taught about Gandhi in my previous life as professor in peace and conflict studies, I also knew that when he returned to India, he went on a year-long journey to see every corner of India and learn how her people lived. So I combined these ideas. What if I walked every street in Winnipeg, to see how my neighbours lived? What if I walked this as an urban pilgrimage? Could I walk like Gandhi, or King, or Thich Nhat Hanh? Could I learn to walk as if each place were a sacred pilgrimage?

I bought a city map, a highlighter, and some refillable water bottles. I set out on my urban pilgrimage. I decided on a few guidelines for myself:

- No electronics—I did not want to be distracted. Phone, iPod, and all such devices would be left at home or in the car.
- No wallet—for a number of years I have felt awkward about mixing money and sacred practices. I had witnessed a number of Indigenous people doing Smudges. They would always take off their glasses, watches, and jewelry before washing themselves in the sacred smoke. I used a similar practice to symbolically take off my shoes to acknowledge that I was on holy ground. I did not literally take off my shoes, because while the ground was holy, it was also cold, since autumn was in full force.

- I would not talk publicly about my journey until I was more than 100 km into it. I loved the idea of the urban pilgrimage but I knew that I wanted to speak from the perspective of practice rather than the realm of ideas. I told my family and a couple friends but no one else.

Beyond these few guidelines, I had no great directions. I just wanted to be present, to walk mindfully, and to enjoy touching the earth.

This was a beautiful time for me. I saw parts of Winnipeg I had never seen. Some days, I would contemplate a quote about walking. For example, I had heard the question: What is the speed of love? Response: Three miles/hr.–walking speed. But mostly, I tried not to fill my mind with too many thoughts and just go and be. This was energizing. At first it was hard for me to let go of my inner world of thoughts and emotions. But as I learned to broaden my horizon of interest, I had the time and space to cultivate relationships with people and places I would otherwise never have seen or met.

I highly recommend you set up your own approach to doing a pilgrimage where you are. If you want more teaching on walking meditation, I recommend Thich Nhat Hahn's, *How to Walk*. Learning to dance with elephants is in part about being on the move in a non-violent, non-harming way. Urban pilgrimage is a mindfulness training that touches on this kind of movement. I hope it will lead to true happiness for you.

Just as I reached the 100 km mark, three things happened that led me to give up my goal of walking every street in Winnipeg. First, I got a parking ticket. This wasn't really relevant, but somehow it discouraged me. Second, Canadian winter arrived. Where we live, the winter temperatures go down to -40 C (also -40 F). Third, we got a puppy, which demanded a different kind of mindfulness training (the subject of the next chapter).

At some points, I felt like a failure. I had set a goal of walking every street in Winnipeg and I did not meet that goal. I had not walked as far as Gandhi's Salt March, which he did when he was over 60. I was 43. My competitive and goal-driven nature was still living strong inside me, and my inner voices told me I was a failure. Looking back, I see it differently, but it was not easy at the time.

Now my focus is less on covering every part of a map and more on simply taking each step in gratitude for life. This is a happiness project. The urban pilgrimage was the training ground that continues to shape who and how I am now.

Find some practice of walking meditation. It will probably look very different from mine. What matters is not how it looks, but rather the spirit you bring to it and your openness to learning to see anew.

{ 10 }

Loving a Puppy

Tabitha prescribed a puppy for my family. Tabitha is an ex-Hutterite and co-owner of Tallgrass Prairie Bakery in Winnipeg. This is the same bakery Kathy Barkman (Chapter 7—Living Beauty Awake) helped start. Tabitha is also a friend and a member of our circle of caregiving friends (see Chapter 12—Responding to a Disease with a Circle). In our community, Tabitha is a bit of an Elder, meaning when she speaks, people pause to listen. At one of the meetings of our support circle (see Chapter 13), Tabitha took it upon herself to prescribe that we get a dog.

Later that night when we told our twin daughters what Tabitha had said, they were very excited. They had an ally. They had wanted a dog for years, and from time to time had tried to convince us. In fact, Sara had been working on a PowerPoint presentation to make her argument! Rhona knew that much of the work would fall on me, so she said it was my call. I am not entirely sure why I agreed. I had no sense that I needed to have a dog, but I respected the people who said it would be good for us.

We ended up getting a beautiful golden lab puppy. Koila picked him from the litter and Sara named him Kobi. And so our family expanded, in ways that none of us could have imagined. Kobi was born in December, 2014. Seven weeks later, we brought him home.

The first year we had some challenges as we slowly trained one another, but by now we are all in love with Kobi. Every day I hear my girls squeal in delight at how cute he is or how much they love him or how they will never find someone more handsome than Kobi.

To be honest, it is not just the girls who squeal in delight. Rhona and I get in our daily share of squeals—much to the chagrin of some of our friends and family.

Wake up—pet the dog, who calmly rolls on his back or leans in for a cuddle.

Go downstairs to let the dog outside and gently give—and take—some love on the way.

Before the coffee is made each morning, we have all participated in multiple acts of love and happiness.

Love is weird that way. It is not like money, which decreases as you use it. Nor is it like anger, which pushes others away as you use it. Love grows into more love.

Having a dog—even a poorly trained puppy—is minute to minute mindfulness training in happiness.

We've noticed this happiness is not contained to our family. Not everyone gets infected with this happiness virus, but as we walk down the street we see faces light up—children's, adults', people of all ages and abilities. I am not sure what people see when they see Kobi, but when he is present, smiles arise all around. It is profound. Kobi is a happiness virus.

Sometimes when people are having a hard time, they will pop into our house for some puppy therapy. Sometimes when the girls experience conflict or anxiety or are mad at their parents, they want to have Kobi around them. He makes us into better people.

There is a quote: "I hope I can be half the person my dog thinks I am." What I like about this saying is that dogs see us through the eyes of love. As long as we don't hurt them and attend to a few basic needs, the dog does not hold a grudge. Each time you walk through the door, he is just happy that you have arrived. And his happiness makes happiness arise within us.

Before Kobi, our family did not have any pets. I know many of you knew about the miracle of pets long before us. If mindfulness trainings are there to train us to love, then having a dog is one of the best mindfulness trainings I have ever experienced.

For our girls, loving an animal so deeply has led them to become vegan. When they saw our meat system as cruelty to animals like Kobi, they radically changed their diets. They recently had their one-year vegan anniversary.

Having a dog has helped us to let go of some fears and replace them with true happiness. A dog—and especially a puppy—is a lot of work. But as we let go of our need to have an always clean house, we have also increased our overall happiness.

To be an elephant dancer, you need to learn to love the elephant. If the elephant is too frightening, start with a dog. If you allow it, your dog will train you to increase your love and happiness.

{ 11 }

Diving into an Ocean of Gratitude with Patch Adams

P atch Adams estimates that, as a clown, he has been at 10,000 deathbeds. I asked him what he learned from being present at these deathbeds, dressed as a clown with toys in his pocket.

"They are not deathbeds," he said. "They are living beds. There are two states: alive and dead. From the second you are conceived, you are dying. That is not interesting—especially since you are also living."

Then he looked into my eyes and said, "Either you're living or you're dead. The fact that you are 'dying'— well, I see you as living. So where is the fun?" It was as if he was saying, you are living so live well and have some fun!

Later in our conversation, I asked him if, given his experience, he could offer a few hints on living well for those of us who are labeled with a disease.

"How many do you want?" he asked. Then he sat back and said, "We all die. Relax. The question is not 'how.' The question is: Are you living? Are you being the human being you want to be? Are your relationships healthy? Are you grateful? What is your sense of wonder? What's your sense of curiosity? What thrills you?

"You can decide to love life. You can decide to love your partner. You can decide to know what I mean when I say that a tree can stop your suffering."

Somehow, those words struck me as freeing. I don't need to figure out everything about dying. I need to keep living. To be thrilled, grateful, wonder-filled and curious about life and living. These are ways of being that are accessible to me.

If someone else had spoken these same words to me, they probably would not have had the same effect. Perhaps if I tell you some of Patch Adams' story, you too will feel a deep surge of gratitude for being alive and you might accept the deep dare to live a life shaped by caring for others.

Some people think they know Patch Adams' story because they saw Robin Williams portray him in the famous Hollywood movie. However, the real Patch Adams is quick to point out that the film profoundly simplified and sanitized his life.

Patch was born in May 28, 1945. He grew up an army brat, following his father around the world and watching as war stole his father's soul. After his dad died, in 1961 during Patch's teen years, his mom moved the family to Virginia. This was a time of open racism. When Patch saw "Whites Only" signs on public drinking fountains, he came to believe that his country was fake and religion was fake because they allowed such injustice and dehumanization. As a teen, Patch was beaten up for standing against violence and racism. Over the course of a year, at the ages 17 and 18, he was hospitalized three times for attempted suicide. Patch did not want to live in world with so much violence and injustice.

It was during his third hospitalization that his life changed direction. For him, it was like a lightning strike: "You don't have to kill yourself. You need to make a revolution, a love revolution."

He was confronted by two questions:

1. *How do I find a love job for men in a capitalist system that is making its people sick?*

2. *How can I be an instrument of peace, justice and care every day?*

The first question set him on a quest to become a free doctor. The second led him to practice clowning every day.

At the age of 18 he says he "dove into an ocean of gratitude and has never found the shore." At this same time, he identified six qualities that he committed to living everyday: happy, funny, loving, cooperative, creative, and thoughtful. He told me, "Since then, in 54 years, I never had a bad day!"

As a young adult, he turned his attention to books and to social experiments in loving, and playing. Through these social experiments, he crafted himself into an instrument of peace. He dressed in many costumes so that he could learn to engage people in theater. Every day for two years, he spent two hours calling wrong numbers to learn how to talk to strangers, trying to keep the other party on the phone. He also rode elevators, 10 hours a week in Washington, D.C., to learn the art of engagement.

For Patch, medical school seemed to teach everything that was wrong with society: elitism, racism, speed doctoring, medicine for money, hierarchy.

The year he graduated as a medical doctor, 1971, he also released an eight-page paper on a model hospital designed for holistic care. He called the model hospital Gesundheit! Institute.

For the next 12 years, a small group of families and doctors lived out a mini-version of the model to demonstrate that it could work.

Here are some of the striking characteristics of this model of care:

- No charge for medical appointments.
- Average patient visit lasts three to four hours, as opposed to the standard seven-and-a-half-minutes.
- All permanent staff live together communally.
- Everyone makes the same salary ($300 a month).
- Patients live alongside doctors and their families.
- No health insurance reimbursement.
- No malpractice insurance.
- Ecovillage environment. Eventually, the hospital bought 321 acres in West Virginia (the poorest state for health care), providing a place to soak in the beauty of nature with three waterfalls, caves, a four-acre lake, a mountain of hardwood trees, and wildlife.
- Organic farming on the premises; Patch was a goat herder for eight years.
- Integration of the healing arts.

When Patch started the mini Gesundheit! Institute, he and his colleagues thought the full-scale hospital would be built in four years, by 1975. Yet over the next 12 years, they did not get one donation. They learned that giving and loving were a kind of high. But they also learned that they would need to change their approach if they wanted to attract funds.

Patch then started to work full-time at outreach and speaking engagements to raise the money for the model hospital, a dream that is yet to be realized. (You can donate here: http://www.patchadams.org/donate/). He spends up to 300 days each year on the road and has visited more than 90 medical universities in 70 countries. Apart from doctoring, Patch finds he needs to have some ongoing way to care for others if he is to sustain his work. So he decided to responds to every letter written to him as an act of care. Further, he decided to make clowning trips into some of the neediest places in the world: war zones, refugee camps, orphanages, prisons, areas of abject poverty, and centers for veterans of war. In each place, he tries to infuse society with the joy of living. He sums up his approach by saying: "My spiritual path is loving people."

When I spoke to Patch over Skype, I saw a 71-year-old man dressed as a clown, with long white-and-blue hair that has not been cut since 1967. In characteristic style, his white mustache was curled up at the ends. He wore a pink-and-purple tie and bright red glasses to finish off the outfit. Across from me sat a man whose dream has not yet been accomplished, even after four decades of trying. But as he spoke, I knew this was an unimportant detail. He spoke with love, not bitterness.

Talking with Patch made me reflect on this question: What if the answer to most of our problems is to make others radiant? When we are not well, so many medical professionals tell us to focus on ourselves. But what if the key to our own happiness is to care for others?

From Patch, I want to learn the joy of living, the gift of living in gratitude, and the deep transformations that arise when we care and love those around us. This book outlines some of my own social experiments in loving, but Patch dared to me go further, bolder, and freer.

In my video recording of our conversation, you can hear Patch share his own story, as well as explore things like how a tree can stop your suffering, why loneliness is the worst human condition, and what tricks you can use to help people love and be joyful.

Part III
True Love

{ 12 }

Responding to a Disease with a Circle

You know the size of an earthquake by the violent impact of its tremors. When my mom was the same age as I am now, the year was 1990. I was in grade 12. We were probably about eight years into the earthquake of her Huntington's disease.

By then my parents' relationship had been crushed, piece by piece. My older brother—protecting himself by doing what I often wished I could do—got the hell out. My mom had already alienated herself from almost everyone. Much of the time, she stayed at home and would not answer the door. I was left alone, with her.

To make matters worse, I tried to be the compassionate, listening son, staying present through the trauma of the earthquake that knew no end. For my mom, those were the days of suicide threats and attempts. It was her I-hate-all-men phase and her eight-year-migraine headache phase and, to me, it was her you're-going-to-be-an-awful-parent phase. She spent most days in her housecoat, on the couch, throwing up into an empty four-litre ice cream pail, the kind she had previously filled with homemade chocolate chip cookies. Her cooking and baking days were behind her now. She was in the fog of Huntington's. We were all in the fog of Huntington's

She was still in denial that she had the disease. And we had 16 years of more earthquake trauma (and other things too) to go until she died.

Can I Stop Passing Down Trauma Earthquakes from One Generation to Another?

Mostly I try not to think about those days. But now I have this disease. Now my twin girls walk the same halls of our neighbourhood inner-city high school where I took refuge when I was their age. For some time now, each time my wife, Rhona and I argue, there is a moment when she looks at me in fear and sees a disease.

I keep wondering what kind of habits and supports could make this walk a little more bearable, maybe even enjoyable, for my kids, Rhona, and me. I am reliving my teen years, wondering what might have helped us during the earthquake. Which ways of living, what kinds of mindfulness training might equip us to live in a way that does not dump all the trauma of previous generations onto the heads of my girls? For me, loving those around me requires that I pursue that question with everything I can give.

I don't think we are ever alone, but as a teenager, I felt that way. In hindsight, I am still a bit jealous of my brother, who, while also caught in the earthquake, was always better at saying "no" and creating some distance. My mom, my brother and I needed support. Our circle was too small. Support was offered many times, but my mom was not interested.

So this time around, I want to try not to make all the same mistakes. I want to widen and strengthen our circle. I have come to believe that people from various cultures have been gathering in circles for a long time. In Canada, gathering in circles to respond to traumatic events is quite common in Indigenous communities. Many of these practices were unjustly outlawed, shunned, and discouraged. But there is still a living memory among some of their elders. They remember ways that the community gathered in circles to try to help people walk in a healing way, to help people understand their identity and the connections to the world around them. I believe such practices were common around the world. Before states stole conflicts from communities, communities gathered together in circles to become strong again.

In my prior life as a peace researcher and teacher, I did a lot of work in the field of restorative justice. This is one of the settings where people around the world are re-learning how to use peacemaking circles to move from crime to community. Living Justice Press is a great book publisher whose single purpose is to share such examples of circle peacemaking.

Circles of Support and Accountability is an organization that powerfully developed circles around people who were incarcerated for sexual offences and who were held until the end of their sentence because of their high risk for reoffending. Keeping these offenders in prison until the end of their sentence actually makes our communities much less safe, as there's no transition and no accountability. People go straight from prison to the community, and because they have served their time, the state has lost the right to limit their freedoms or hold them accountable. Circles of Support and Accountability steps into this problematic situation. The organization has helped stop cycles of harm while helping some of the most problematic offenders find themselves again while surrounded by a community of care. The circle tries to offer support with reintegration into the community while at the same time creating accountability by challenging behaviour that might lead to more harm.

This example has been a model for me as I have considered how best to widen our circle and protect my family from the effects of the Huntington's earthquake.

One of my greatest fears with Huntington's is that I will harm my own family, following the pattern of my mother. Having spent my life exploring healing ways, I know that circles have great transforming possibilities.

As a family, we created a circle of support and accountability as a reference point for the journey. We picked six people from our church with whom we had a very positive relationship of respect. We chose people with the following traits:

- people with whom we could share freely;
- people from whom we would welcome support;
- people we allow to call out our bullshit; and
- people we welcome to help shape our family.

One of the things I like best about my church community is that through hard-won experience, the group tends to respond to traumatic events by creating circles of care. At life-stage changes, like turning 12, becoming married, and having children, the church gathers more naturally. But a similar approach is used for traumatic events: a breakdown of a marriage, the dying of a friend, deep conflict between members.

It is not a rule or requirement or even an expectation. It is simply done because people have witnessed firsthand the goodness that comes from sharing in each journey, especially at those most painful places of disorientation. So when a dear friend (and circle junkie) from our church offered to do whatever we wanted to make such a circle available for us, we agreed. We had already been talking and planning for such a circle.

We invited the carpenter, the artist, the baker, the psych nurse, the social worker, and the food justice advocate. I know, it sounds like a joke. But for us, these are simply our friends. Everyone said yes, even though each had many good reasons to say no. They are our companions. Right now, we gather every other month, alternating sharing circles and meals with kids. The carpenter facilitates.

Right now, we share our journey and build relationships of trust with every member of the family. We have also invited our circle to ask hard questions. Most nights turn into a conversation. Our friends have decided to educate themselves about Huntington's disease by going to conferences. One night we brought in the social worker for the Huntington's Society in our province. We discuss each member of the family and what support might be helpful. So many of my medical doctors are specialists in one part of my body. But the circle is different. This is holistic, offering support for the whole family. In time, they will hold me accountable to walk in a healing way. The work we do now has much to do with what they will be able to offer later.

The Wisdom of Circle Responses to Traumatic Journeys

I hope that sharing this journey with our circle of support and accountability takes some of the pressure off Rhona, my kids, and myself so that there is more space to enjoy the road ahead.

It seems to me that circles teach us a lot about living life with wisdom. So far, here are some of the gems I've learned:

We need one another. We often cannot heal or walk in a good way all on our own. We need communities of support and care to help remind us of our identity amid our disorientation.

Rather than trying to battle disease and trauma, circles provide a way to care for your disease, as if it were a crying child.

We respond to entrenched disagreement (the stuff we refuse to budge on) by eating meals together. Eating together is a sacred act.

You may be surprised by the kind of support that people are willing to give, if offered a concrete option like a circle. The gift of the circle extends outside its borders. Our twin girls both have jobs at the bakery that the Baker co-owns. Each month, we go on date night with a couple in the circle. Good things tend to happen as people are given permission to care.

When our circle first started to gather, our supporters were very aware that they did not know a lot about Huntington's disease.

In passing, we said that the national conference on Huntington's was coming to our city and that Rhona and I would go and see what we could learn. Without our knowing, members of the support group went to the church and asked for money for the whole circle, including us, to go to the conference to learn about Huntington's Disease. The church approved. Everyone from our circle signed up. When we all showed up for one of the main sessions, we filled a whole table! I should say we almost filled a table. One chair was left empty. Soon, someone we didn't know came and sat with us. We introduced ourselves. When our new friend learned that the whole table was from our church, and there for Rhona and I, she was shocked. She is a social worker who works for the Huntington Society of Canada. She commented several times on our odd arrangement. She said most individuals don't even get this much support from their family, never mind the wider community. That stuck with me.

Healing resources are out there. We often fail to find ways to access them. Creating a circle of support and accountability has benefited our lives. I am curious how others have created ways of accessing and engaging the communities around them to become circles of support and care. I encourage you to think of ways you might tap into the wisdom of the members of your circles.

When I got sick, a lot of people said, "If there is anything you need, let us know." I think they meant it. They didn't quite know what to offer and we didn't quite know what to ask. The circle gives us space to ask for specific help, but even when we say there is nothing we need right now, the response is always, "Don't wait until we gather again. Just call us."

For us, this kind of circle of intentional friends provides an ongoing way to face life with all its twists and turns. I hope you act on finding the wisdom resources of walking in a healing way.

{ 13 }

Dying and Mourning with Love

We have been taught—by so many voices—to fear death. And yet death is so profoundly human. It is one of the few sacred tasks all humans share: birth and death. Often, but not always, it is these basic sacred tasks that unite humanity: breathing, eating, peeing, pooing, birthing and dying. Elephant dancers need to learn to perform each task with compassion and love. We need to resist the culture of fear and anxiety at each step. In fearing death, we often miss out on living and loving. Elephant dancers can use the dying of loved ones as mindfulness training on how to live and die well. Perhaps by learning to unlock the keys to dying, we will create the space to keep learning to love.

How do we unlock the keys to dying well? Here are some of my insights from mourning and celebrating the life of my mother-in-law, Kathleen Hildebrand, who died peacefully on September 22, 2016.

Does Every Death Need to Be a Tragedy?

While I was doing my master's degree in peace and conflict in Virginia, Rhona and I worked at a retirement community right next to the university campus. We were on call evenings and weekends to help residents deal with emergencies. Over time, we started to learn what was important to residents. They would often speak of dying. More specifically, they would speak of their hope to die quickly and relatively painlessly. For them, a quick death was living the dream, the best way to go.

When I reflect on the residents at the retirement home, I wonder about those who got their wish. I wonder if their families felt the freedom to celebrate this dream death. Generally, when someone dies we feel that we need to respond to the death as a tragedy. "I am so sorry for your loss," we say to mourners. And indeed, there is loss and sorrow that comes from death. But surely not every death is best labeled a tragedy. How do we create space to celebrate dying well, as a natural part of living? How do we let go of the idea that something was unfairly stolen from us?

Letting Go of Heaven

In Kathleen's last days, what did she fear? What made her anxious? In my view, one of things that made her anxious was her view of heaven, where she would be reunited with two husbands - the first had died of leukemia decades earlier and the second had died of cancer just three years ago. For her, the idea that she would die and go to heaven was not entirely a comforting thought—would she have to choose between husbands? This wasn't the dominant theme in her last days, but seemed to me to be consistently present.

As a Christian who has a degree in theology, I do not believe in a heaven that you go to when you die. I think that is a very dangerous idea that is not actually found in the Christian scriptures. This idea of heaven creates fear and anxiety for many people, and these are not the fruits of the spirit. The idea of heaven as a family reunion needs to be explored much more deeply—when was the idea invented? By whom? Who benefited from the idea? When it was put into practice, did the neighbours of Christians experience it as the fruits of the spirit: love, joy, peace, forbearance, kindness, goodness, faithfulness, gentleness, and self-control? If not, then the idea was likely not from God or from love.

It pained me to see Kathleen feeling confusion and anxiety about heaven when she needed her focus elsewhere.

The Power of Laughter, Tears, and Silence

Laughter, tears, and silence came like healing waves in the hospital room. They came again at home, at the viewings and at the funeral. This was a gift-the kind of gift that comes as family and community are present to the dying of a loved one. One of the many things I deeply love about my in-laws is that they are very comfortable engaging in all three sacred practices together: laughter, tears, and silence (not necessarily in that order). I think one of the keys to dying well is creating space and giving permission for these three healing friends to do their work.

The Wounded Healer

What did Kathleen care about? What was she curious about in her last days? I can't know with certainty, though I am bold enough to reflect on what seem to me to be the likely answers. After Kathleen died, I went to her condo. This was the week we were all supposed to help her move from condo life to assisted living. On the floor of her living room were empty boxes for moving. Of course, these would now be used to take away her last possessions. Her condo was not overflowing with clutter. Mostly, what remained were pictures of family.

I went and sat on her couch. On the coffee table were the TV remotes she could never figure out how to use without help. But the coffee table was mostly clean save for a book. I unthinkingly picked it up to see what she was reading. Knowing I was in a rural, conservative Bible-belt, I was not sure what I would find. I read the title, *Living with Huntington's Disease (A Book for Patients and Families)* by Dennis H. Phillips. She was reading about me! I flipped through the book—published by a university press in 1981. My mother-in-law, who was losing her vocabulary, was spending her last days trying to learn about my disease and what her family might be experiencing. In classic Alzheimer's style, she had kept reading and re-reading the same short section of the book and would then relay her "new" learning to other family members, again and again and again. But this moved me. Her attention did not focus for too long on herself. She was trying to help others. She wanted to understand me and my family.

This theme arose again later in the week when my wife and her siblings had to decide which charity they would ask people to donate money to in lieu of flowers. I was not at this meeting but was told afterward that the family wanted to pick something that reflected what Kathleen was interested in at the end of her life. They decided to ask people to donate to the Huntington Society of Canada. These were my in-laws who did not have Huntington's in their family, but as a last act of loving-kindness and sharing, they were asking people to donate to what might support my family. What a surprising act of kindness! It came in the midst of mourning, at a time when you wouldn't expect a family to reach out to support others!

Now when people say, "Sorry to hear about Rhona's mom-how are things?" I want to explain my deep sense of awe and gratitude, but in the moment words fail me. Perhaps I too am losing my vocabulary. I hope Kathleen's compassion and curiosity will guide me on this path.

{ 14 }

Loving Our Ancestors

Our ancestors have much to teach us. In most cases, in addition to passing on wisdom, they may also have passed on trauma. Often, before we can benefit from them, we need to work on seeing our ancestors through the lens of compassionate understanding and, often, forgiveness. If we are going to work at loving our families, we need to look through the eyes of compassion at how they were trying—and sometimes failing—to dance with the elephants in the room.

You can see for yourself one of the best examples of this kind of generational healing in a video called Hollow Water

https://www.youtube.com/watch?v=MMKIvv5p164

(4min and 49 seconds into this piece). The people in this community were some of the most inspiring people I've met in my travels and research around the world. Hollow Water is an Indigenous and Metis community in my home province of Manitoba. The people of Hollow Water were trying to interrupt the cycles of violence by focusing on sexual abuse—which had touched between 66 - 80% of the community. The video shows one of the first couples they worked with, and you'll see how they created a family tree of abuse as part of the healing process. Hollow Water is all about taking responsibility. They have learned to shift from blaming the individual; to instead, healing through the generations.

A great energy and focus arises when we learn that our task is to make sure the cycles of harm and abuse are not passed down to future generations.

I have experimented with applying this approach to my own healing journey. I worked back five generations. I think it would be great to go back seven, if I had that information. One of the insights of our Indigenous people is that to understand the violence now, we need to look back seven generations, and when deciding how to act now, we need to act in ways that benefit seven generations to come. I love this view.

I examined my family of origin, moving backward this way:

First generation: my children (and their future children)

Second generation: my siblings and cousins and I

Third generation: my parents and their siblings

Fourth generation: my grandparents on both sides of my family of origin

Fifth generation: my great grandparents

Then I considered the kinds of traumas they faced and the kinds of traumas they imposed on others. This will be different for every family, but here is my list.

SA = Sexually abused

PA = Physically abused

MA = Mentally abused

S = Suicide

SA = Suicide attempts

AO – Abused others

FG = First-generation immigrants (left a homeland)

IN = Institutionalized in asylums for the insane

ED = Eating disorder

D = Disease

A = Addiction (alcohol/drug abuse/gambling)

W1 – WWI

GD = Great Depression/Dirty Thirties (1929-39)

W2 = WWII (1939-45)

R1 = Voted for political parties that support genocide of Indigenous people in Canada (Canada recently concluded a National Truth and Reconciliation Commission of the genocide treatment of its Indigenous peoples from 1876-1996.)

R2 = Would have a problem with their own child marrying someone from a different race

W = Treated women with less respect than men

WFB = Witnessed a family breakdown

WA = Witnessed community violence-atrocities

WT = Witnessed terrifying and perceived-to-be life-threatening event(s)

MH = Mental health issues

EP = Experienced poverty

DI = Divorced

Then I thought about each person in my family and tried to create a family tree of trauma. Of course, the tree is missing all sorts of very important information because there are lots of traumas that people do not speak openly about. But this tree does not need to be perfect in order to be healing.

Next, I tried to add as many of the indicators that I knew about and I asked relatives if they knew of other traumas experienced by our family. This process was very moving. Although I had intended to share my family tree with names removed, I've decided to keep it private; even without names, it involves other people's stories that are not mine to share. But the point of this tree is to be inspired to break the cycles of violence and trauma instead of passing them down to the next generation.

Thich Nhat Hanh often addresses the topic of healing your ancestors. When I was at his community, each night they would practice Touching the Earth—a practice devoted in part to your ancestors. You can reflect on some of Thich Nhat Hanh's words by watching this video:

https://www.youtube.com/watch?v=2hg0CWwMvM8 &t=145s. ("Touching the Earth" from Thich Nhat Hanh's book "Happiness

While I was in Plum Village, I modified this practice to fit my life. I had not yet made my family tree, but this is what I did: I went for a walk of healing for one ancestor at a time. It was important for me to touch the earth. In his book, *Happiness*, Thich Nhat Hanh says, "While touching the earth, breathe in all the strength and stability of the earth, and breathe out to release your clinging to any suffering." The earth is a healing helper. On each walk, I found a rock that I could hold in my hands to represent one of my ancestors. I walked slowly, thinking only about this ancestor.

- *What was your life like?*
- *What traumas did you experience?*

- *How did you see your other family members?*
- *What made you afraid?*
- *Who taught you fear and violence?*
- *Whom did you harm?*

Of course, we need to also ask about all the positives, but starting with their traumas helped awaken and open my heart toward them. So, with no real plan, I walked. Asking questions. Listening quietly. Sometimes I would go through the decades of that person's life. Sometimes I would breath in the strength and stability of the earth and then breathe out sufferings. When I found my mind racing with thoughts of unrelated things, I simply stopped walking. When I refocused, I took another step. This practice was not about distance or time, it was simply walking in a healing way with my ancestor. When I felt like I was finished, I would clutch the rock in my hand and make sure I was touching the earth: bare feet, sitting or lying face down. I said a prayer: "My dear ancestor, I know you suffered deeply. I bless you and wish you well. I let go of the suffering that is passed down through the generations so that our future generations will thrive with compassion. My dear earth, please take these toxins and turn them into flowers." Then I would leave the rock in that spot. For me, this was very freeing. I do not mean to say that I am free of suffering passed on from past generations—I do have a genetic disease. But now I also have more compassion and greater happiness. Priceless.

The world is learning more and more about generational trauma. These practices motivate me and equip me to not pass on as much of that trauma to future generations.

A related concept, but highly unexplored, is that of generational blessing. What are the blessings—the good things—that our ancestors passed on to us? What are the good things we will pass on to the next generations? But that is a topic for another time.

I have laid out for you how I am trying to work at five generations of healing. I don't have time to be frozen in bitterness by what the previous generations did or did not do. Healing is about letting go of the things that cannot give life and daily doing the things that can. The healing practices that work for you may well look quite different from the ones that work for me. But I do want to dare you to work at healing your ancestors.

{ 15 }

Playing with Children

During the opening ceremonies of the Canadian Truth and Reconciliation Commission, I went to the sharing circle focused on the abuse that had taken place in residential schools run by churches and the government. There was an old Indigenous grandmother there. She came into the circle clutching the arm of a younger white woman. When the grandmother got up to speak, still clutching the arm of the young woman, she said, "I am so grateful to be able to draw on the energy and power of the younger generations. I do not know this woman but I must draw on her power to say what I must say today."

For me, children are just like this. Simply being close to them, perhaps even touching them, gives me energy, happiness, joy, love, and a will to live. Playing with children is a mindfulness training that leads to love. I have always liked kids, but now their presence is even more meaningful. In a social situation, if I can choose between playing with kids or talking to adults I don't know well, I will always choose the kids. Yes, for me this is the easier path, but it is more than that. Playing with children creates new, refreshing energy. When we are close to a baby, we can feel their gaze before we even touch them. Feeling their presence, we soften our own gaze. When they smile, we smile deep inside. Like some crazy quantum entanglement, we feel what they feel even if we are at a distance.

I adore my two teenage daughters. I probably get into more arguments with them than anyone else in the world. Of course, we each think the other is the source of the disagreements. And now there are more times when I get angry, which is a subject for another chapter. I mention this here just to say that we have all the ups and downs of the parent-child relationship, plus we must figure out how to relate to this elephant in the room called Huntington's disease. So life is complicated. Sometimes we completely miss each other. But I still adore them. I delight in them. I can't believe they came from me. When I hear one of them laughing out loud at some show on the internet—maybe even a show I would not choose for them—their laughter, most of the time, brings me deep joy.

Giving birth to children who might inherit a traumatic illness is controversial and needs to be thought through. In fact, with Huntington's disease, not having kids is encouraged by some. When we were in the United States and Rhona was pregnant, we were asked if we wanted to test the twin fetuses for the marker for Huntington's Disease, in which case we could abort the kids. We said no. There are now other options, such as implanting only fertilized eggs that do not have the Huntington's Disease gene. I understand the reasoning. If you could stop this trauma from being passed down through the generations, why wouldn't you? But for me to accept that logic, I would have to conclude that it would be better if I hadn't been born, which would mean that our daughters would not be alive, either (we don't know whether they have the gene or not). But I have loved living. If my life ended today, that would have been enough. And knowing that there are hard years ahead, it is still good. I love that my kids have also been able to live life. Even if their lives were cut short, radically short, I would not regret the life they lived. This is not to pass judgment on choices that work for other people. I am just saying that I am in love with my kids and I am deeply grateful for the life we have had and continue to have together. I draw energy from my kids. When I see how my daughters and nieces and nephews are living, I am emboldened to live well.

{ 16 }

Being Disarmed by Joy with Lucy Kalanithi

From Lucy and Paul Kalanithi, I need to learn how to be disarmed by joy. Paul died in March 2015 at the age of 37. A neurosurgeon and neuroscientist turned cancer patient, he spent his last year writing *When Breath Becomes Air*, which Lucy completed for him. The book has sold over a million copies since its release in January 2016.

After interviewing Lucy, I went for a long walk on the frozen lake near my cabin. I call it walking on water. It is here that I am sometimes able to hear the whispers of wisdom. Soaking in her story, it suddenly struck me: This is a story about being disarmed by joy.

Lucy Kalanithi is a medical doctor, Yale graduate, author, mother, twin, caregiver, widow, and Stanford faculty member. After her husband died of stage 4 lung cancer, she ensured his manuscript was published and wrote an epilogue. *When Breath Becomes Air* has been on *The New York Times* Best Sellers List continuously since its release. Did I say she is in her thirties?

When Breath Becomes Air offers lessons on living and dying with love and integrity, and should be on the core reading list of anyone who wishes to dance with elephants.

When I talked to Lucy, I asked why she thought the book had sold over a million copies. What resonates with people? What surprises them?

"The book is not only about dying. It is about living," she said. "Paul talked about this idea that life is not about avoiding suffering. People have been intrigued by our decision to have a child while he was terminally ill. When we were making that decision, I said to Paul, 'Don't you think having to say goodbye to a child will make dying even more painful for you?' Paul said, 'Wouldn't it be great if it did?' He was getting at that idea that holding joy and pain at the same time is a task for a lot of people. It is a task for all of us, really, at one point or another in our lives."

I know this to be true. Each time I share my story, I hear back from strangers who tell me that learning about my experience with terminal illness helps them to face surprises in life. The source of their challenges is different from mine. They wrestle with loneliness, the disorientation of age, caring for a parent with dementia, or even living with their kids. And yet we feel a connection that transcends our situations. I think we are connected because we are finding a good way to hold the joy and the pain together.

Lucy and Paul each seemed to have learned that there is a freedom in not trying to avoid suffering at all costs. That freedom is the freedom to live fully—not giving up, not just passing time, not withdrawing from life. The freedom to fully live is the willingness to experience deep joy even if it might be mixed with suffering.

Deeper into our conversation, Lucy told me, "I do not think Paul died feeling like he was losing everything. Paul died feeling like he had everything." He communicated this kind of joy for life that does not demand more. Paul worked on his manuscript until a couple of days before his death. His final words in the book are addressed to his infant daughter, Elizabeth Acadia. Those words powerfully communicate this deep, radiant joy that does not hunger for more. Lucy recited them to me:

"When you come to one of the many moments in life when you must give an account of yourself, provide a ledger of what you have been, and done, and meant to the world, do not, I pray, discount that you filled a dying man's days with a sated joy, a joy unknown to me in all my prior years, a joy that does not hunger for more and more, but rests, satisfied. In this time, right now, that is an enormous thing."

Paul was disarmed by joy. He was willing to taste joy, even if it led to great suffering in dying. And, to his surprise, he found a well of joy that was so quenching that he was never thirsty again. His joy came from beholding another with whom he was well pleased. Elephant dancers need to practice daily this kind of beholding another for which inextinguishable joy is a side effect.

It seems to me that for Lucy, being disarmed by joy took quite a different path. Paul's disarming joy, Elizabeth Acadia, is now in her terrible twos. While Paul rests, enfolded in the ground, Lucy and her daughter face life after Paul.

Lucy told me a story that I think sheds light on her different but similar path of being disarmed by joy. The Day of the Dead is a Mexican indigenous celebration, which Lucy said she did not want to misappropriate, but that she found so striking and so helpful. This is her story:

"The year Paul died, we were at the cemetery where he is buried. It's really beautiful there, overlooking the Pacific Ocean. On the Day of the Dead, the cemetery is a very active place of mourning, celebration, and participation. They have these tents for face-painting for the children and sugar skulls, like *calavera* skulls that you can decorate. They have a Mariachi band and a taco truck. It is very striking to see that stuff in a cemetery, with all the colours and the paper flowers. There is just this intense juxtaposition of literally eating a taco while visiting Paul's grave and having all these kids around. It felt true to my own experience of life after Paul's death. The grief and loss and the memory of Paul and the pain of losing him were mixed with my continued love for him and the fact of life itself in all its colours. It is all blended together. I love that holiday."

Paul's unarming joy was a joy rooted in the life of another. For Lucy, joy comes from being able to see and respond to life's strange mixture of colours. Life did not unfold according to Lucy's dreams and hopes. But she is not bitter or angry or feeling like life is unfair. In fact, she is quite delightful to engage. I think she, too, is disarmed by joy. Disarmed by the joy of being able to see life for what it really is, to mourn for that which needs mourning and to celebrate the rich colours of life, sometimes in the same breath. This is a heart whose door is open. When compassionate eyes see life's joy and pain, the one disarmed by joy can still smile.

Lucy reminds me of a favorite poem by Thich Nhat Hanh, "Please Call Me by My True Names." This is just the end of the poem:

> *My joy is like Spring, so warm*
> *it makes flowers bloom all over the Earth.*
> *My pain is like a river of tears,*
> *so vast it fills the four oceans.*
> *Please call me by my true names,*

so I can hear all my cries and laughter at once,
so I can see that my joy and pain are one.
Please call me by my true names,
so I can wake up
and the door of my heart
could be left open,
the door of compassion.

This poem is my prayer for all elephant dancers.

In my video recording with Lucy, she explores non-judgmental loving, rule-breaking, end-of-life care, the battle metaphor, the complexity of marriage and terminal illness, and other mindfulness tools.

Part IV
Loving Speech and Deep Listening

{ 17 }

Refusing to Battle My Disease

Battling disease seems like a bad idea to me. The idea that waging a battle against my body will someday lead to health strikes me as crazy. Why would we wish war on someone who already has a disease?

When I was told I had a terminal disease, the responses of my friends were telling. I know they were in mourning and that they had a deep desire that I would not have to walk this path. So many of them would say things like:

"Fight it."

"Find a way to get rid of it."

"We can battle this together."

"We will use all the weapons at our disposal."

They spoke from the heart and I took their words as a kind of lovingkindness. But now as I continue on this road which some call chronic and fatal illness, I look back at the words of my friends and see that they are filled with military metaphors. Even the health care professionals spoke in the language of violence:

"...a misfolded protein is invading your body."

"Hopefully, research will eliminate the disease."

"Perhaps by destroying rogue cells..."

How strange! Just when I needed help to walk in a healing way, the people around me are turning to the language of war and violence. Now, this is not just my strange friends (though they are strange). This language of violence is everywhere in our communities. But something in me knew that metaphors of war would not help my journey of healing.

Those learning to dance with elephants need practice in deep listening. Not all the voices around us orient us to live in a reconciling and healing way. Sometimes even the voices of friends and health professionals unintentionally prod us down a path that cannot lead to health.

This chapter focuses on the mindfulness training of deep listening—listening for what lies beneath the surface, listening to distinguish that which can lead to good living from that which can't.

I did a little digging online to see who is thinking about this odd and pervasive "battle" perspective on disease and dying. The best I found was an article in the *Atlantic* titled, *The Trouble with Medicine's Metaphors* by Dhruv Khullar, M.D., a resident physician from Harvard Medical School. After surveying research on the topic, he concludes that military metaphors might cause more harm than good. What an understatement! Here are eight reasons I refuse to battle my disease (or use the language of war to find the path of love):

1. Battling My Disease Is a Losing Battle

With Huntington's disease, there is zero possibility of "winning the battle." The same is true for anyone with a fatal illness. I don't mean to alarm you, but all of us are in the same boat, as life is a fatal condition. We all "lose the battle" at some point. We are all supposed to fight but we are all losers! How is this helpful? Even just war theory says that a war cannot be just if there is no possibility of success. This is a war we should not be fighting.

If the choice is between winning or losing the battle, I am losing the battle. But I reject the choice.

I don't want to spend my limited energy fighting or battling anything. I want to enjoy the path.

2. Battling Disease Doesn't Work, Even for Those Who Win

People who "win" the battle with disease often still consider themselves losers. As more and more people "survive" cancer, some of the "survivors" are rejecting that label. They feel that the term does not shed light on the many ways they are still affected by cancer and its treatment. My wife's cousin is one such person. In fact, she is working on a handbook to support people who have survived cancer but have not been able to return to their previous level of functioning. More research is coming out on this topic. Livestrong's research shows that 98% [of cancer survivors] experience continued physical, emotional, and practical concerns. Yet many did not receive help for their needs. Even in actual wars, we are finding that soldiers who've "won" the battle have high rates of suicide, PTSD, depression, and domestic violence. If that's what winning the battle looks like, I don't want any part of it.

3. Disease Is a War Without an Enemy

Medical studies show that those who approach their disease as an "enemy" tend to have higher levels of depression and anxiety and poorer quality of life than those who ascribe a more positive meaning. They also tend to report higher pain scores and lower coping scores. I used to teach peacebuilders how to diminish their enemies by not cultivating them in the first place and by loving them in the second place. It is remarkable to me now to see medical scientists make the same claim about health! Enemies are not good for us. If I must battle my disease, I make an enemy of my body. No, thank you.

4. Battling My Disease Feeds Denial

"Your mom took denial to a whole new level." These words came from my Huntington's disease health team. My mother had only one tool: denial. For those of us around her, this denial created a wake of misery. I vowed not to repeat that pattern. Over the years, I have developed a nose for sniffing out denial. I have learned that I need to be careful when people tell me that I should be free of this disease. I try to receive these comments as good wishes. But if I let myself, I can start thinking, *maybe there is a way to get rid of this. Maybe some prayer, some action, some science...will free me.* For me, the path of denial leaves an empty space where misery can grow, especially in those around me. If I pretend I don't have the disease or that I will get rid of it, then I pay less attention to living each moment with care. For me, the battle image feeds denial. I think this is very dangerous for my family.

5. Battling Disease Is Inspired by a Violent, Colonial, Macho, Paternalistic View of the World

Shortly after Justin Trudeau was elected as Prime Minister of Canada, he was asked why his cabinet has an equal number of men and women. He responded, to the cheers of crowds, "Because it is 2015." In the same way, I feel it is passed the time to be done with the violence, oppression, and discrimination embedded in our culture. There is something about the European-Caucasian way of being that has allowed violence and oppression to touch every aspect of our lives: in medicine, politics, theology, and criminology. *Uhh, let's find the problem and kick the shit out of it. Uhh, let's kill the Indian in the child. Uhh, God demands bloody punishment. Uhh, what criminals need is more pain and suffering.*

Canada recently had a Truth and Reconciliation commission. We agreed to work to get rid of the very imagination that inspires the grotesque ways we relate to Indigenous peoples. The path of reconciliation must include exploring how violent oppression informs all areas, including medicine, politics, theology, and criminology. So, what does an approach to medicine look like post-Truth and Reconciliation? We must let go of find-problem-and-kill-it medicine. We must let go of violence-inspired medicine. Battling my disease is not for me. I put my hope in embracing dustness.

6. Battling My Disease Serves as a Blinder

Nobel Prizes have been awarded to scientists for rejecting a strictly mechanical understanding of life. The machine metaphor was a huge blinder for them. With the blinder removed, they could make revolutionary advances in fields such as neuroscience, quantum physics, and organizational leadership. Likewise, our assumptions about the need for violence blind us to the wisdom of old and the wisdom yet to come. We miss the wisdom of other traditions. I'm letting go of the blinders and looking for wisdom wherever I find it.

7. Battling My Disease Does Not Help Me Practice Loving Speech or Deep Listening

Those of us trying to practice loving speech and deep listening know that the way of violence does not lead to the way of healing, particularly in situations where the potential for violence already exists. Increased aggression is a very common symptom of Huntington's, especially for men in the first stage of the disease. The incidence of domestic violence is a lot higher than average in Huntington's families. So far I have not done this. But this increase in aggression is not unique to Huntington's. It is very common with many mental health issues and chronic conditions. If we are going to stop traumatizing our families with the fallout of violence and aggression, we need to stop promoting violence to tackle disease. Rather than telling me to battle a disease, ask me how things are going with practicing loving speech or deep listening. I need this mindfulness training to protect my family.

I hope I have made it clear that the battle metaphor seems completely unhelpful to me. Dancing with elephants seems to me to be a better a metaphor, one that allows us to engage with that which we fear without adding more violence to the equation. We need to do everything we can to avoid the way of violence. Cultivating deep listening, loving speech, and a dark sense of humour can help. We also need the support of our friends, families, and health professionals to avoid the path of violence while at the same time cultivating a more healing path.

{ 18 }

Naming Your Own Way

One evening several years ago, when I was putting one of my then nine-year-old twins to bed, she looked up at me and said, "Dad, why do they call it Huntington's disease?" I responded, "What do you think they should call it?" She said, "Huntington's disease sounds too scary. They should call it Starburst." At the time, I leaned over and said to her, "Well, if they called it Starburst, everyone would want to have it!" We had a good laugh. At a young age my daughter knew the power of claiming the space to name our own experience, despite what doctors might tell us. This was not the first time I had learned this lesson.

Naming, done well, is an overlooked and underused mindfulness training for elephant dancers. It is a form of loving speech that arises from deep listening.

They Call Me a Rape

Years ago, a rape victim taught me a similar lesson about the power of naming. Rob Baum's poem powerfully communicates how naming creates and defines experience. Here are just two lines:

> *They call me a rape*
> *but I say it was done to me*

The criminal justice system begins by naming the harm according to its own standards and not according to the experience of the victim. "They call me a rape." The victim is sidelined, or, as Rob Baum's poem goes on to explore, "neatly transcribed and tucked in sweet dreams amid the files...already I am textbook material."

Sometimes I feel like the sidelined victim given the external label, objectified, and struggling to find space to define my own experience. I don't want to be considered nothing more than my disease. I want to name my own experience, rather than taking the definitions of the medical field. I am not against the medical sciences. I know that, like many others, I stand to benefit from them. However, I don't want to be robbed of this important task of naming my own experience. If my daughter knows the deflating power of being called a disease, I should not think I can ignore this insight without causing more harm.

The First Sacred Tasks

In the Christian sacred texts of my own tradition, the first tasks of humanity were breathing, eating, and caring for creation. I think these sacred practices are often overlooked, especially in most Christian traditions. But it is the next sacred task that caught my imagination. According to this creation story, God sees that humans are bored. God seeks to create partners for humanity and creates all the wild animals and invites humanity to name them. This is not the kind of naming intended to control or dominate. It is much more sacred and intimate. It is the kind naming that allows the namer to be freed from boredom by recognizing the connection, distinction, and partnership of the other. It seems to me that this is more like the way I name my lover than like the way a Lord might name his subjects. Perhaps this kind of love-naming should be a core practice for living. What would a community, or even a person's life look like if it were formed by these sacred tasks: breathing, eating, caring for creation, and love-naming?

If I were to guess the lessons in the creation story for me, I would think that claiming the right to love-name my own path and experience might be important. "Being a disease" might cut me off from community. *He is not normal, not like us.* Being labeled with a disease might create a dis-ease of loving partnership. In the creation story of my tradition, isolation, boredom, being cut off from community, and lacking loving partnerships are all part of the problem because they do not orienting us toward a healthy way of living in the community.

What Do You Do for Work?

I have not yet found a good answer to this question. Usually I tell people I am on long-term disability; sometimes I tell them I used to be a university professor. Most people respond with regret, awkwardness, and sometimes sympathy. I don't blame them. It is like they fell into a trap. One of the key ways we get to know people is by asking about their job. But what about those of us who can't work? Sometimes I take some delight in how people squirm when I mention long-term disability. Some even take a step back, perhaps trying to protect themselves in case what I have is contagious. Other times I get caught in my own feelings—it is like the walls go up and I get cut off from friendship. Curiosity is replaced by pity. What am I going to do with all this pity?

Then I noticed that naming my career as long-term disability is like letting others name me a disease. These are frames of reference for my life which seem to be leading to pity, despair, and disconnection. What are my options for re-framing? How could I name my situation in a way that leads to healing?

Here is one option:

New friend: Jarem, so what do you do for work?

Jarem: Well, it is a bit embarrassing! A few years ago, I won the lottery.

New friend: Wow. How much?

Jarem: $1.14 million (that is the sum of my monthly disability payments over 25 years, which is the upper life expectancy for someone with Huntington's disease)!

New friend: Do you want to party?

Pity is replaced with partying! What a transformation. Lottery winner or long-term disability? Hmmm....

I like how winning the lottery is rooted in part of the truth and re-frames disability toward living life. However, there is a lot that I don't like about the winning the lottery answer—it reduces life to money, it denies the difficult journey ahead, and it doesn't help the people around me to engage in the journey I am on.

I don't yet have a name for this journey. For me, right now, elephant dancing works. This task is deeply personal. It is my hope that each of us keeps naming and renaming the journey of stumbling toward a more healing way.

{ 19 }

Making Friends with Darkness

Your uncle spends most of his time huddled in darkness, in a quiet room with a thick blanket covering his body.

I have been unable to get that picture of my uncle, in the advanced stages of the disease, out of my mind. How do I prepare myself for this future?

Once you decide to embrace darkness, a different world comes into focus. I find this world more mysterious and more beautiful. Most of life begins in darkness. A seed falls into the ground, and dies. This is where life begins again: in the darkness of the soil. Light is important. We could not exist without the sun. But darkness is also important. We cannot exist without it. Plants can't exist. Babies can't be born. People can't sleep. Life as we know it would end if we had no darkness. So if we look at the soil or at the womb of a pregnant mother, we see that we need the warm embrace of darkness for life to flourish.

Now when I think about my uncle, maybe he was returning to the womb. In a fetal position, encased in the womb of a blanket, he lies in the stillness of the dark. Huntington's disease returns you to infancy—limbs moving involuntarily, completely dependent. Some Indigenous people say that old people have this tendency to return to the fetal position—that is why they walk all hunched over.

Experiments in Embracing Darkness

I have taken on some experiments to help me reframe the memory of my uncle into something more positive. I have been working at readjusting my approach to darkness. If you would also like to experiment with darkness, here's how you can give it a try:

Sit in complete darkness and silence for 30 minutes at a time. If you must think about something, think about the womb and the ground you return to after death. Extend as you wish. Repeat as necessary.

Or lie in bed in the fetal position, under the covers, in complete darkness and silence for 30 minutes. If you must think about something, think about my uncle craving this still darkness. Repeat as necessary.

There are some things that can only be experienced in silence and darkness. Now I anticipate sitting in darkness. It feels like it enfolds me. I can feel the hairs on my skin relax as they receive the darkness like a thick blanket. Overstimulation is everywhere. To me, it feels like strong wind on raw flesh. But darkness and silence have become good friends of mine. I can reside in darkness. I can build a home in darkness. I can abide in darkness. In this stillness, I find my home.

Perhaps I understand my uncle now. Beneath it all, there is a deep yearning for peace. But it is more than a yearning. A yearning marks the absence of something. Those who have made friends with darkness and stillness know my uncle discovered a way to experience the fullness of peace.

{ 20 }

Remembering Forgetting Is OK

One day I lost my wallet—three times! Each time, I retraced my steps to try to find it. I found it once in the Safeway parking lot. I must have looked like I was searching for a bomb as I ran around the parking lot looking under cars.

I found it another time in a great little local grocery store. One of the employees who was outside having a smoke saw me doing my car-to-car bomb run and asked what I was looking for. He was leaning against a fence just off the store's property. I told him. He pointed at the fence post. My gaze turned up from the parking lot to see that someone had neatly placed the wallet on the post. I am grateful for smokers.

The third time, my wallet had fallen out of my pocket while driving and slid under the driver's seat. That was all just in one day. No joke. No, nothing was taken from my wallet.

I am not only talented at losing wallets, I am also good at losing iPhones. I think I've lost my phone three times now, though not all in the same day. A couple of times, Rhona received texts from random strangers telling us where to pick up the phone. I'm learning this is a good way to meet the neighbours. One time, a woman said she found my phone right in the middle of the street by the local elementary school, just after school was let out. One time, I lost it with the battery dead. After a couple days, I used "find my iPhone." It was in a store I had been to earlier that week. The employees noticed the phone was dead so they charged it just in case someone tried to figure out where it was. Each time, it has been returned in perfect condition. Oh, yeah, there was another time I left it out overnight in the rain. That one died. Now our family rule is that I get the oldest hand-me-down phone we have.

I am not bragging. I am just trying to show that remembering is an hourly activity for me. Sometimes I succeed. Sometimes I don't. Before I was sick with Huntington's, losing my wallet would upset me and throw me for a loop. But with Huntington's, my view has changed. Now, instead of going into a rage, I get to meet the friendly neighbours!

At some stage, my forgetting could endanger my health or the health of those around me (e.g leaving an stove element turned on). At that point, I still think forgetting will be okay but I will also need to trust my community of caregivers when they say it is time to make different living arrangements. I've recorded this hope in this book, so in the event that I forget, please just show me this page!

If I am going to have to work through anger, frustration, and anxiety every time I forget something, I will have no time to do anything else. I do not want my days to be full of anger.

So if you see me touching myself oddly when leaving the house or walking down the street or coming out of the store— know that it is not what you think. *To try to not forget*, I tell myself. *Remember the trinity.* Then I touch myself, doing what might look like the sign of the cross: wallet, keys, and phone.

When I do forget, most of the time I am going to be kind with myself. I can smile and say there is more of that to come. When others forget things, I tell them we are part of the same club.

Now, for some, finding themselves forgetting is a painful thing. I know what it is like to wonder if your forgetfulness is an early symptom of something more serious. For Rhona's mom, part of having Alzheimer's meant that she forgot all the time. Forgetting was one of the few things she would remember to do. But that was fine. She would usually say, "I should remember." I always wanted to shout out, "Stop 'should-ing' yourself. Your brain is not working." Memory comes and goes. Ironically, the more angry or anxious you get, the worse your memory works.

So, whatever you are facing—be it aging or traumatic disease or some other elephant—please pledge not to fill your days with anger by getting mad at your memory. The people around you do not need your anger. They need your loving presence.

{ 21 }

Breathing Anger

Anger is something I wrestle with. Ask my daughters or my wife. They know that sometimes I get mad and it takes quite some time to cool down. To make matters worse, anger has not traditionally been my thing. It is in the last decade and a half that I have had to wrestle with anger.

The problem is not anger itself, but rather the ghost of my mother. Her ghost haunts us. I don't mean I've seen some version of Casper the ghost. I mean that hollow silhouette that my mother became still haunts us. If you were to ask Rhona what she fears, what her elephant in the room looks like, she would tell you that she fears me becoming like my mom. Or at least the person she got to know when were married, nine years before my mother died.

As Huntington's disease progressed within my mother, she started to fixate on things that made her angry. For example, when our girls were born in 2001, my mom learned that we had given Sara the middle name of Rhona's mother. She decided it was not fair that our other daughter, Koila, did not have her name. This led to months of agony for all of us, as my mother would leave 25 messages in a day, on my work phone, demanding we legally change the name of our daughter.

Anger +Fixation = Agony

Sometimes, I get jealous of the people around me who don't come from Huntington's families. Many of them get angry but don't have to worry about being haunted by a mother with Huntington's. But when I am more clear-sighted, I see that anger is a toxin for all of us—those of us with Huntington's Disease and those without.

In the hopes of learning more about letting go of the toxins of anger, I share here the practices I have been experimenting with.

Time Outs for Breathing

It used to be our children who got the time outs. Now it is me. I give myself time outs. When I can feel the temperatures rising, I explain that I need some space and go up to my room. This does not always solve the issue but gives me space for perspective and breathing. Sometimes

I lie on my back on the floor and try to practice mindful breathing. Sometimes I can slow down and even enjoy taking breaths of life. Then the joy of life and breath tends to dissipate the anger. Others times, this does not work at all.

Mantras

Thich Nhat Hanh taught members of his community to use mantras to remind themselves to act with compassion when doing everyday things. For example, before starting a car, the monks and nuns are supposed to say, "When the car goes fast, I go fast." It is a kind of reminder to act responsibly with the car. Incidentally, at least one of the nuns—the one who picked us up from the train station—seemed to see this mantra as a dare to go crazy fast. Mantras probably work best when you make them for yourself. Mine have changed over time. At one point, when I was regularly getting upset, I set out to create a mantra. The only one I could come up with was, "I will not return evil with evil." It is a line in Christian scriptures which speaks to not returning violence with violence. To be honest, though, part of what I liked about it was that I could still imagine that whoever I was mad at was doing evil to me and I was going to act better than them. This mantra was a judgment of others and was certainly not ideal, but it did help me through a rough time. I would use it to remind myself that I was not going to add anger to anger. I never said it out loud.

Here are some other mantras I have used over time:

We have bigger fish to fry.

How do you want the girls to remember you?

How can we be guided by loving speech and deep listening?

These can be helpful when they act like little bells reminding us to be loving to those around us.

A Cabin by a Lake

We've only had the cabin a little over a year. I know this is not financially possible for most. I share it because it has been fantastic for our family. We have a place where Rhona and I can go at the drop of a hat. In a year's time, when the girls are driving, they may also decide they too need an oasis of beauty where they can soak in sustained times of silence, reflection, and darkness. For me, the quiet and the darkness at the cabin feel like being soaked in healing balms.

Do Things that Create Joy and Love

We each need to regularly do things that create joy and love within us. If we want to offer joy and love to one another, we need to build up some excess love. Ask yourself and the people around you, what actions create joy and love within you? Pledge to make sure to do those things regularly. Everyone will be happier.

Listen for the Symphony of Creation

Go outside. Taste the air. Touch a river. Find some grass. Stand in the presence of the trees. It can do wonders for you.

Anger and Power

When I was first getting to know Ovide Mercredi, a Cree and a former National Chief of the Assembly of First Nations, we went for a long drive to talk, mostly so that he could poke and prod me, to see if we were a good fit. One of the things he taught me about on that first drive was anger. He said he was working with young Indigenous men to move beyond their anger. He explained that they had a right to their anger. Anger is a right response to injustice. But what he had to teach them was that every time they expressed their anger publicly, they lost their power and their voice. The public sees "just an angry Indian," he said. He was trying to teach them to see what lies underneath, deeper than anger. I know when I get angry, I too lose my power and my voice. Rhona and the girls most often think my anger is a Huntington's symptom. Every time I let my anger out, they don't hear my words or my concerns.

Reflecting on Ovide's insights about anger led me to write this poem:

The Freedom of Non-Entitlement

Beneath some of my suffering lies anger
Beneath anger, impatience
Beneath impatience, entitlement and wrong expectation

Entitlement is the seedbed of wrong expectation
Expecting now what cannot be now creates impatience
Impatience erases time and creates anger rooted in the
injustice that our wrong expectations cannot be lived
now
Anger overflows to suffering
The suffering of wrong thinking and
The suffering of wrong action
The presence of this kind of suffering
waters the seeds of anger, impatience, wrong expectation
and entitlement
And the cycle of violence goes on

Transform entitlement and a new horizon of being
Bubbles forth into the present moment

Through the law of non-entitlement
we can embrace and enjoy death
The ones who know

the universe does not owe them anything
are free
A great weight is lifted
We are not entitled to our entitlements
They are not what makes us beautiful

The flower follows the law of non-entitlement
It does not expect to live without end
It does not see its own death as injustice

Gazing at the flower we know will die
Does not feed within us the seeds of anger
Somehow suffering diminishes
in the presence of the flower's fragile beauty

How can I live and die
Like the presence of the flower?
How do I embrace the way of non-entitlement?

{ 22 }

Practicing Awe During Winter's Creep with John Paul Lederach

John Paul Lederach is one of the most accomplished scholar-practitioners in the field of conflict transformation and peacebuilding. He has spent his life trying to help others walk in a more healing way. Eight years ago his wife, Wendy, was diagnosed with Parkinson's disease.

In my search for a more healing and loving way to face disease, I needed to seek out someone who understood my approach to peace, conflict, and change while at the same time understanding the challenges and gifts of a long, slow, progressive disease. I knew I needed to seek out John Paul, who was one of my favorite professors when I was completing my master's degree at Eastern Mennonite University in Virginia. When Wendy was diagnosed with Parkinson's, I was dealing with learning that I would get Huntington's disease. There are a number of similarities between the diseases, including the slow decline toward death, which can be as long as 25 years. I wanted to see what they were learning about facing disease.

John Paul is the author of more than 20 books on conflict transformation and peacebuilding, including one published by University of Oxford Press. What I find more interesting about him is that his work took him to places like Nepal, the Philippines, Columbia, West Africa, East Africa, Nicaragua, Northern Ireland, and Spain. He often stayed involved in these places for decades. He is a modest, engaging, and profoundly curious person who does not shy away from the complexity of life. He even has a sense of humour. For example, he likes to point out that he used to specialize in church conflict but that was too hard, so he moved to settings of long-term violence.

Wendy, I've known only from a distance. She cofounded a Ten Thousand Villages retail store in Harrisonburg and ran her own jewelry line later with artisans in the developing world. As far as I could tell, she was a ball of positive energy and a good person.

I was delighted when John Paul agreed to let me interview him for my video series. After some warm words, he jumped right in. Here are a few snippets:

The hardest learning curve I've ever had.

It is like a new landscape you've never walked.

It comes into life unannounced.

It is not easy.

We're floating in a world that is less than visible.

I have failed amicably and I am still learning.

I've discovered that my well was not very deep.

This is not a disease that is a lightning strike like cancer. It is like winter creeping in.

It's like a slow violence, kind of like climate change. We all know it is there but because it is slow and the time frame is large, we don't notice and respond as we should.

I liked hearing these words. I do not take joy in the pain felt by another, but I take comfort in honest, open reflection. My teacher was not going to pretend to have all the answers. He did not hold himself up as a perfect caregiver for Wendy, even as wanting to be a good caregiver.

Winter had come for them. And as in the TV show *Game of Thrones*, winter is not about to go away anytime soon. All the peace and conflict transformation skills could not hold off winter. But one of the things John Paul and I share is the knowledge that peace is the way we struggle. Peace is not the absence of the storm. Peace is not some tranquil, idyllic place. And peace does not keep winter at bay. But peace names the way we struggle with that which lies before us.

We discussed what helped and what did not help from our academic field and from our shared Mennonite background. John Paul added to something we had observed: many of the practices of faith communities are held in communal settings. When it is hard to be around large groups, communal acts no longer serve those facing this kind of disease.

Then he offered me a gem. John Paul loves telling stories, so here he is in his own words:

> *Faith is also about a sense of awe that is captured in the mystery of the extraordinary gift of life and the world we were born into. Nature often brings that for me. So a lot of my faith practices have been less communal and more about an in-depth conversation or through the daily dose of vitamin awe. We need a daily dose of vitamin awe. We tend to see awe as something that we experience once a year. We go on vacation. But think about what you did this morning. You told me you "walked on water this morning"* [walking on a frozen river, at -40°C/F with my dog]. *That tells me you are a*

person who has been nurturing your daily dose of vitamin awe. I don't know why we don't have that as a core practice. To be very honest, if I experience awe in the congregational setting, it is almost always around singing. Singing together is something that captures awe, and it has always been there. When we're singing, we lose sight of all our differences, which really is an amazing phenomenon.

I think one of the big challenges is how not to become callous or cynical or bitter.

Callous means you do things that just keep the pain at bay—you're not going to be touched by this thing. Cynical means that you might use all sorts of defenses to avoid going very deep into how painful this is. And bitterness comes when you know how painful it is and you are angry.

I don't think there are a lot of remedies for the winter creep other than vitamin awe. With vitamin awe, everything pops open and becomes alive again.

Cultivating awe is a form of mindfulness. Awe is there and present in almost everything around us every day, but we so rarely touch it.

I left the conversation feeling hopeful. This isn't a hope that arises out of ignorance or wishful thinking. There is a much stronger hope that arises when we learn how those living in winter find ways to delight in the present moment. Going to church may no longer work for me. However, John Paul points toward the practice of seeing and responding to awe every day. Even I can do that.

Wendy's emails always come with a signature line: "When you stumble, just make it part of the dance." In some ways, she is teaching people the same practice of cultivating awe. We cannot stop the stumbling. But if we are not filled with fear, we can make the stumbling part of the dance. Awe is still available, amid the creeping of winter.

In my video recording with John Paul, he reflects on the gift and challenge of slowing down, becoming an artist of change, being surprised by impatience, sustaining curiosity, poetic listening, and the gift of quality presence, which he calls "alongsideness."

Part V
Nourishment and Healing

{ 23 }

Embracing Weakness

"We have heard nothing from you for six months. What has happened? Has your disease made it impossible for you to continue to write? How are you? Are you doing okay?" These are the questions I have received from my friends when they haven't heard from me in a while.

Don't cry for me, my friends. I have been enjoying practicing the embracing of weaknesses—more specifically, how to rock tunnel vision. While the "successful" strive for an endless stream of multitasking, I have been (re)exploring the one-thing-at-a-time method. Aging and my Huntington's disease have combined to strip me of any illusion that I might be able to multitask my way to anywhere.

In the "normal world," people expect multitasking. We are expected to get things done while at the same time responding to waves of emails, Facebook posts, phone calls, tweets, newsfeeds…

But I have been learning to lean into what I saw as my weakness and that which I feared. I have a one-track mind. And I am celebrating it. I have a deep, burning desire to focus all my attention on one thing until it is finished. Rather than fight this, I experiment with living into it. I have completed a number of big tasks this way: painting our cabin, creating a book and a blog, refinishing the kitchen, redoing hardwood floors. However, to do this, I have had to ignore everything else. I don't respond to friends and family. I don't pay bills. I don't clean the home. I avoid all social settings....

Elephant dancers need to embrace weakness if they are to flourish. Therefore, I am sharing with you four secrets to rocking tunnel vision - or whatever it is that you fear within yourself.

1. Make Friends with Your Enemy

The Huntington's doctors don't speak much about tunnel vision, but they have their own way of naming that experience. They speak of compulsive behaviors and obsessive, intrusive thoughts. They say the holes in the frontal lobes of my brain are making some important tasks more difficult: organizing, prioritizing, controlling impulses, self-awareness, initiating and ending activities.

But I think this is a fear-based way of seeing my life. The focus is on the negative, on the loss. Battling this loss is a battle that can never be won. So instead, I try to tell my symptoms:

- I am not going to treat you like an enemy.
- I know you.
- I am you.
- You are welcome here.

Rather than treating my symptoms as an enemy invading, I try to welcome them as a friend. Making friends with enemies is about letting go of the horizon of fear so that a new, more healing horizon might emerge.

Whatever you are afraid of in yourself, address it, name it yourself, welcome it, and replace fear with compassionate curiosity.

2. Practice Laughing at Your New Friend

Fear leads us to fight, flight, or freeze. But these are not good ways to build friendships. Learning to laugh is often a better strategy.

We are taught to see the downside of our symptoms. The practice of laughing at your symptoms moves in a different direction.

Laughter creates a playful space to welcome your new friends who will accompany you in this part of your life. If I was fighting or fleeing from tunnel vision, I would not have the capacity to laugh at it. Once I decided to make friends with tunnel vision, laughing was a necessary practice. This is what I like doing with my other friends.

Tunnel vision is one funny dude. Learn to see it and respond with laughter–not with the laughter of mocking or the laughter of giving up but with the laughter of recognizing the goodness in a friend. For example, I have to use tunnel vision to complete this book. It takes lots of energy and I can't really focus on anything else. Recently, I got a phone call about my disability insurance. In a very friendly manner, the agent said that in the last months, I had not returned any paperwork and was in danger of losing my benefits unless I got the form in immediately. I explained about tunnel vision and apologized. He said I could have a month. I told him I had better do it right away, because if I waited a month, there was no way that paper would be returned. We laughed together. I hung up and started filling out the form until I got distracted along the way…

3. Unleash the Benefits of Weakness

Those of us who are losing our minds often try to hide, mask, or manage our symptoms. But they can't be hidden. To lose your mind in style, lean into weakness. Ask your new friends what they can teach you.

What practices make this weakness flourish with goodness?

Tunnel vision does not allow me to do multiple things at the same time. If multitasking is my only definition of success, I will always fail. I need a new measuring stick.

Tunnel vision allows us to deeply touch one speck of the universe. If the entire universe is present within each grain, then tunnel vision (seeing the speck) needn't come at the expense of a more expansive vision. Tunnel vision allows me to touch the whole universe by being truly present to the speck.

4. Protect Yourself and Your Family from the Downside of Your New Friends

Part of the gift of having a hereditary disease is that you can learn how previous generations lived with it. I speak not just from the perspective of someone with a disease, but also from the perspective of one who tried to be a caregiver.

My mom loved tunnel vision and this sometimes had a devastating impact on those of us around her. When she focused on something, she could tear apart anything that got in her way. Remember the story of her wanting us to rename my daughter Koila and the 25 phone calls a day?

I share this story to remind myself that if I befriend my symptoms, I need to learn to do it in a way that protects my friends and family. In other ways, befriending symptoms is about dissolving fear, not about transferring the fear to those around me. Sometimes when we are full of fear, we pass it on like a virus. Elephant dancers need to dissolve fear. My mother knew how to use tunnel vision but she did not know how to dissolve fear. Therefore, she often tried passing the fear on to my brother and me. As elephant dancers we have much to learn about the practice of dissolving fear.

{ 24 }

Falling Mindfully

Practicing Mindful Falling

Walking my dog in the winter, I discover new ways of falling and bruising myself. Most winter mornings, Kobi and I walk five minutes down the street from our home to one of the frozen rivers that cut through our city. Kobi loves to run free-range in this unofficial off-leash park.

Now, to picture the scene, you need to realize that the disease I am facing is, in part, a movement disorder. If you haven't seen someone with Huntington's disease, you might imagine someone with full-body Parkinson's disease on steroids. Lots of erratic, involuntary movements. I'm at the beginning stages, but the nature of involuntary movements is that I cannot control or completely trust my body.

So you can imagine walking on snow and ice trying to hang on to a Golden Lab puppy is sometimes quite a funny sight. Lots of falling. Sometimes it feels like the dog and I tap dance our way down the sidewalk for the entertainment of our neighbours. I love the quiet, peaceful setting of the frozen river and a smaller audience to watch my dance.

Recently, Kobi and I were doing our morning river walk on an icy surface. There was also a light dusting of snow, making everything extra slippery.

When we got to a part of the walk with uneven ground, of course, I fell. I fell backwards on my ass, elbows, back, and head. I am not sure what I said as I was falling. I am trying to embrace falling. If I am going to enjoy life, I must figure out how to enjoy life with falling. I've wondered if falling can be like a mindfulness bell, gently calling my attention back to the incredible gift of life. On this day, I fell hard. I lay still, alone on the ice. I scanned my body. Felt alright. So I stayed on the ground. I knew I needed to make friends with the ground. Cursing it won't help me much. So I lay still on the ground and thought about the gift of life.

Just at this point, a man with a dog came down to the river and saw me. In an instant, my mindful falling was forgotten. I realized I've become that strange man who falls on the ground and doesn't get up. What's wrong with him? I was flooded with memories of Mom with Huntington's disease. Or more specifically, of people talking about my mom. "Yes. I saw her in the park and had to help her up out of a snow bank," I remember them telling me. And I started to see how they saw her: *What's wrong with her? Who sits in a snow bank? Why doesn't she have socks on? Should she be outside?* And I started to see how I saw my mom: *What's wrong with her? Why can't she remember to put proper clothes on before going out? What do the neighbours think?*

All these thoughts flooded my mind as I lay on the ground. Not wanting to be looked at the way people looked at my mom, not wanting to be looked at the way *I* looked at my mom, I jumped up from the ground.

I started to talk to myself in my mind. *Screw making friends with the ground. I look stupid. Get off the ground. Get on two feet and look normal.* I'm sure that the worst way to "look normal" is to heap shame and embarrassment on yourself and then to try to force being normal, whatever that is. However, that did not stop me from trying. I met a new neighbour, Erwin. He was very good about it. Kind in every way. This made me angry at first. Deep down, it made me embarrassed. It is hard to fall mindfully and it is even harder to fall mindfully in front of others.

Falling by Myself

In my experience, falling when no else is around is easier than falling in the presence of others. So falling by yourself is a good place to start this practice. At first when I fell, even by myself, I would get angry. I would smack the ground with my fist and curse. But now I laugh at the thought of me smacking the ground cursing. The ground did nothing wrong. In fact, no one did anything wrong. One of the things I have learned from mindful falling by myself, is that I must discard any notions:

- of blaming
- of naming wrongdoing
- of " should-ing" myself (I should have done…)
- of shaming myself
- of being embarrassed of who I am and what I am doing
- of guilting

For me, those notions lead to anger and self-hatred. I need to find ways of falling that lead to loving, not hating. If I keep practicing this kind of angry, hating falling, I will *become* anger and hatred, and this will deeply scar those closest to me. I must learn a kind of mindful falling that leads to love.

An early way of working at mindful falling is to meditate on the picture of yourself falling angrily, until you begin to laugh. Laughter is the process of letting go of that part of the self that wants to hang onto the impossible, and live in a world without cause and effect.

A next step is to listen to your inner voices when you fall. Pay attention to them. Ask where they came from. Ask if you want to give those voices power over you. Stay on the ground until you can honestly say, "I do not blame the ground; I do not blame myself. Letting go of blame, I love the ground. Letting go of blame, I love myself." These words may not work for you. Find your own words. But every time you fall, use the experience to learn to love yourself. This will also do wonders for the people around you.

Falling in the Presence of Others

I find this one much harder. As a student and as a university professor, I became very good at the art of impressing others. I was deeply rewarded for this art and became addicted to it. It is that addiction that hurts me when I fall in front of someone like my kind neighbour, Erwin. I want him to like me, to affirm me. Who affirms a falling person?

As humans, we do not seem to like falling or fainting. It sometimes even traumatizes the bystanders. We do not like to see people out of control. Perhaps the falling person looks like the person is dying. Maybe our bodies reject falling as a knee-jerk safety mechanism to avoid perceived life-threatening situations.

When I fall and lie still on the ground, I know I am not in a life-threatening situation. But others don't. We know how hard it is for others to see us out of control, and so we get up as fast as we can to make it better for them.

In truth, I am just a beginner at the practice of mindful falling in the presence of others. I find it hard to picture it in my mind's eye and smile at the situation. I am not yet laughing. I have much practicing to do. I think if I can embrace falling in front of others, this will decrease fear in me and perhaps also in them. Fear calls out more fear.

But I don't know what it takes. What should I have done when my neighbour Erwin called out to see if I was OK as I lay on my ass on the frozen river? Are there ways to use this kind of falling in the presence of others as a teaching door that leads to love? I think so.

Next time I fall in the presence of others and am asked if I am OK, I hope I stay there on the ground and say, "Just practicing falling in love."

{ 25 }

Valuing Your Life

What is your life worth?

This is the question an Indigenous Elder has been asking me again and again over the last several months. If the question came from a financial planner, I would know how to answer. I would know the intent behind the question. But this Elder lives in economic poverty. In my experience, the wisest Elders don't talk too much about money. He must mean something else.

Each time I reflect on the question of what is my life worth, I come up with one answer: dust, a grain of the universe. As I learn to dance with elephants, I have found that I must turn toward my fears and my mortality. In the chapter "Embracing Dustness," I reflected on Gandhi's words: "The seeker of truth must be humbler than dust." In the chapter "Replacing Fear with Love," I outlined a practice of meditating on your bones turning to dust. So my answer may be in part because I have been thinking about dust, but I believe there is more to it. For me, dust is a key to nourishment and healing.

By saying that my life is worth dust, I am not saying it has no worth. To me, dust is one of the most valuable things on this earth. Life is made from dust and returns to dust and becomes life again. How miraculous is that? Remove dust and there is no life. Life crumbles to death and death crumbles to life. For me, it is not the life or death that I find difficult. Instead, it is the process—which all of humanity is embarked on—of crumbling.

I wrote the poem below, in part to challenge my own faith tradition to take dust more seriously. I wrote this as I travelled back from a sabbatical as part of my work as a university professor. That year, I had been to Sri Lanka, Papua New Guinea, and Israel, visiting communities with some practice of healing justice. My family and I had just lived for six months on Saturna Island, a secluded island on the West coast of Canada. Rhona and the girls had travelled ahead of me back to Winnipeg. I wrote this poem on the 25 hour drive home. I knew my career and professional life would soon end, and I was mentally preparing myself and my family for the journey ahead.

On this Sacred Earth (or Going Home)

On this sacred earth
I will not curse your name
I was created for life
I was created for death

And all the crumbling in between

When I die
Don't let the crazies say I passed away
or went to some better place.
I died.
Let me go home to the earth
Where folded in silence
I can return to the dust
From which I came
Death is not some evil dominion
Where the Devil and Darth Vader mate
Death is life's consequence
Together named Very Good
In the sacred earth
Come what may

On this sacred earth
I will not curse your name
I was created for life
I was created for death
And all the crumbling in between

While I still live
Don't be swayed by fortune-sellers
Promising a better life in some other time or place
If we want to touch the sacred gift of life,
We have but one access point:

Each present moment on this sacred earth
Let me go home to the earth
Where surrounded by beauty
I can learn to love and let go
Life is not some place to escape
Where sorrow and fear dictate
Life is a sacred gift
On this sacred earth
Come what may

On this sacred earth
I will not curse your name
I was created for life
I was created for death
And all the crumbling in between

It's not the living or the dying that I fear
It's the space in between
Not living, not dying,
just hanging on
destroying all I meet
When you find me crumbling in between
Remind me to behold the flowers and sparrows
We behold these sacred beauties because they wither
and die
Behold the dying flowers; there are no other kinds.
Their withering nature is how they were created to be.
Let me go home to the earth

Where we all live in between
Let me go home to this sacred earth
This dying, living, crumbling earth
Come what may

{ 26 }

Eating like a Buddha

Eating together is one of the most sacred tasks. To share a meal is the ultimate expression of friendship and trust. In every major life event, we turn to food as the backdrop to make sense of our lives. Birthdays, weddings, funerals, anniversaries, sporting events, major holidays, romantic evenings… all incorporate eating together as part of the celebration.

It is no wonder that when working at nourishing, healing, and reconciling, we turn to food. Go to a bookstore and you can see that the cookbook section is far bigger than sections on spirituality or even business. We love our cookbooks. Perhaps because we are food. No cell in our body would exist without it.

Eating is a vital part of elephant dancing.

We all know food is important. What we can't agree on is what is good to eat. Each cookbook claims to offer recipes for the best kind of food. A hot new diet is as common as a passing cloud. So how might elephant dancers eat in such a way that leads to nourishment and healing?

I am of two radically different minds on this.

Part I – Eat like a Fat Buddha

I love food. I look like a fat Buddha, and eating like a fat Buddha is something I can share with full integrity. Eat like you will die tomorrow. Savour everything. Eat like you are losing your mind. Now, I agree this might not be the best advice for mindfulness training, but there is something mindful about not sweating the things that will not matter in 200 years. Your weight likely won't matter. Your lunch choices this year probably won't matter a whole lot in 200 years. Our family tries to buy local and organic, but that is not easy in a Canadian prairie that's frozen more often than not. We try to avoid toxins and consume that which nourishes.

In our house, we have a tradition of "party night." We'll take any excuse to celebrate life. Party night includes nice food, drink, and sometimes inviting friends or family. We don't wait for birthdays. Party night can happen multiple times per week. During my first year in forced retirement, I decided to cook my way through a fantastic cookbook one day each week. We invited friends to join us. All they needed to do was pitch in for the grocery bill. Once a week, I served up the best meals I could muster. Great fun.

Life is richer when our basic stance is reverence, happiness, love, and nourishment. I don't know how the fat Buddha got fat. But probably not from eating a minimal diet. If your basic attitude is to celebrate, you might become, like me, a fat Buddha. It is not an accident that the fat Buddha is also called the laughing Buddha.

Part II – Eat like a Thin Buddha

This second way is more difficult. It is probably closer to the way I think I should be eating. When we see eating as mindfulness training, we must ask the question: How can we eat in such a way as to avoid toxins and to nourish and heal? I know I will not eat my way out of Huntington's disease. I also know that the healthier I am, the better it is for my family.

My daughters eat like thin Buddhas. They are a year into being vegan. This journey began for them when they fell in love with our puppy (see chapter 10). Out of respect and love for animals, they decided to become vegan. I am proud of them. I don't eat the same way they do, but I admire their deep commitment to making their eating habits consistent with their best insights on love. This is fantastic.

Our teenage twins say that Rhona and I don't stick with any diet and just jumps from one to another. There is some truth to the claim. Here are some of the cookbooks in our house that have survived many rounds of purging:

- *Eat Fat, Get Thin: Why the Fat We Eat Is the Key to Sustained Weight Loss and Vibrant Health* by Mark Hyman
- *The Wahl's Protocol: A Radical New Way to Treat All Chronic Autoimmune Conditions Using Paleo Principles* by Terry Wahl
- *The Four-Hour Body* by Tim Feriss
- *Practical Paleo* by Dianne Sanfilippo
- *Mediterranean Paleo Cooking* by Caitlin Weeks and Diane Sanfilippo.
- *Oh How She Glows Cookbook* by Anglea Liddon
- *I Quit Sugar Cookbook* by Sarah Wilson

Our current focus:

- *Quick & Easy Ketogenic Cooking* by Maria Emmerich.

These books share some things in common. Decrease or avoid sugar. Eat fats to fuel the brain and mitochondria in the cells. Avoid processed foods. Decrease gluten, grains, and legumes. Eat organic. If I would stick to these rules, I would probably look more like a thin Buddha. Perhaps I would feel and think more like a Buddha too.

So why am I of a split mind on this? First, I don't buy into the idea that "living the good life" means living as long as I can. Second, these diets tend to be very expensive and aren't sustainable for most families. Third, these diets don't work well when eating with lots of different people. I don't expect others to cook differently for me. I want to share meals with friends and families. If we were to strictly follow these diets, it would have an impact on our relationships. Fourth, these diets are work and sometimes I just want easier options.

I need to eat like a Buddha, but I am still exploring what that means.

{ 27 }

Developing a Family Health Plan

While we are dancing with elephants, we need to guard against turning the elephant into the main attraction. I want to dance well with Huntington's. But I also want my family to thrive. Too much focus on me or on the disease could quickly put us out of balance.

Creating a present and future family health plan has let us love rather than fear. We can plan for the life we want to live rather than wait until the last minute and respond out of fear.

Denial, waiting till the last moment, and responding out of fear was characteristic of my mother. During transitions, she would panic, and too often had to choose between bad options. When it was time to move out of her condominium and into a care home, she refused. She was unable to keep up with cleaning, cooking, or taking her medications. She also kept firing the people who were there to help her live at home independently. So we had to go through the process of getting her declared incompetent. No child wants do that to a parent. That was a deeply painful part of our journey. I remember sitting on the edge of her couch as the doctor took her through basic questions which she had no ability to answer. Time of day, day of the week, year, the Prime Minister's name, three words he had asked her to remember. At first my mom thought she was doing well, but by the end, even she realized she did not have answers. When the doctor explained to her that she would need to go to a nursing home, she had a kind of turning point, right there on the spot. "Well, then I will go and make it the best place possible." I was grateful. But some of the light in me went out that day. It was a necessary step in her care, but the step did not have to be so traumatic. I know firsthand as her caregiver that this last-minute, fear-response health plan was an awful way to live. I vowed to never do that to my loved ones.

I want to chart a different path. Some decisions will be very hard for my family to make for me. I want to be involved early so that I can use the wisdom that has come out of these mindfulness trainings for elephant dancers.

Here is what we have done as part of our Family Health Plan:

- We have created a circle of support so the weight is shared more broadly (chapter 12).
- We wrote our wills.
- We made sure the family is protected from me if/when I start making bad financial choices. Our concern was what would happen if Rhona died when I had more advanced Huntington's. I would become the beneficiary of her insurance and benefits at a time when I could make some very bad decisions. We set up Rhona's estate as the beneficiary. Then we created a spring trust to handle the money for our girls and me.
- Rhona was given power of attorney.
- Rhona got a credit card so that she has credit independent of me.
- We continue to work with a money coach (http://moneycoachescanada.ca/) and an accountant to make sure Rhona and the girls will be provided for in the future.
- We work to ensure that our home is an oasis of nourishment and healing. We try to buy organic and fair-trade. Our furniture is natural wood. We cultivate beauty and purge clutter.

- We make it a priority for me to get lots of sleep every night, even if it means walking out on house guests at 9:00 p.m.

All this elephant training is important because we need to look clear-eyed into the future and figure out how to act in love. If I am still filled with fear, I will cling to that to which I should not cling. I will make life miserable for myself and for everyone around me.

As elephant dancers, we can frame our future major issues within a mindful approach that is rooted in reverence for life, true happiness, true love, loving speech, deep listening, nourishment, and healing. That will look different for each of us. Here is how I outlined my health plan and the questions I need to consider:

- I want a happy family and therefore I am happy to take any medications as needed.
- I want our family's financial situation to be secure; therefore, I do not need to be involved in the day to day decisions. My mother wouldn't answer the phone because multiple collection agencies were after her for the credit cards she maxed out on the shopping channel buying fur coats that she never wore. I am happy to have someone else look after our finances. We have, for the first time, an accountant for taxes.
- I want our family to be healthy and happy, so when keeping up with domestic cleaning gets

too complicated, we will pay others to help us. I would rather be out some money than constantly fighting over who cleans what.

- I want to keep my family and community safe. My car is just a car and does not represent my freedom. I like driving and our latest car purchase was an automatic rather than manual so that I can keep driving safely for longer. But when is it time to stop driving?
- Out of love for my family, I do not want them to do daily care for me in the last stages. Therefore, what nursing home do I want to be in? Likely in Stage IV—typically 11-26 years from onset—I will need to be in a care home. How will we know when the time is right? How can we make that placement an act of love?
- My goal is not to live as long as possible. Therefore, at what point is it a good idea to not treat further health problems? At what point is it right to issue a no tube-feeding, do-not-resuscitate directive?

It does not sadden me to deal with these issues. I want to enjoy my life. I also want the people around me to enjoy life. So I need to address these issues from my present perspective. To me, it is freeing. When fear is not present, there is space and freedom to explore and to live. We can waste energy wishing we were living someone else's life, but the life I have is the only one I can live. I don't want to waste it. Nor do I want to harm those around me. I still have living, loving, and laughing yet to do.

{ 28 }

Mandela Gardening

Being diagnosed with a terminal disease sharpened my vision. As a professor, I had hundreds and hundreds of books. I gave them all away, save a handful. I kept a few extraordinary books that I hoped might still provide nourishment and healing in this part of my life. One of those extraordinary books is Richard Stengel's *Mandela's Way: Fifteen Lessons on Life, Love and Courage*.

I have always felt a deep connection to Nelson Mandela. For me, simply hearing his voice and seeing him on TV were profound experiences. On February 11, 1990, I skipped school and stayed home to watch the release of the man who spent 27 years in prison and who would become South Africa's President and guide to dismantling an apartheid government.

Richard Stengel helped Nelson Mandela write his autobiography, *Long Walk to Freedom*. In the process of writing the book, Stengel and Mandela became friends. But when the research and writing of the book were done, Stengel said, "It felt like the sun going out on my life." Stengel's *New York Times* bestselling book, *Mandela's Way,* was written to share with us the wisdom, generosity, and light of Mandela. I required my Peace and Conflict Studies students to read the book when I taught a course called The Art of Peacebuilding.

One of the many things that stood out for me was Stengel's descriptions of Mandela's gardening. In the 1970's, Mandela started a garden in the Robben Island prison. In 1982, he moved to Pollsmoor Prison, where he created a rooftop vegetable garden using oil drums cut in half.

This is how Stengel describes it:

- While others were playing games, Mandela was gardening.
- He shared produce with prisoners and guards.
- He quieted his mind.
- Surrounded by death and decay, Mandela found a place to touch beauty.
- Gardening was life-affirming and creative.
- This was not a retreat but a renewal, and helped him sustain his work in service to others.

I find these images so powerful. In the midst of death, life! Out of neglect, beauty. Out of misery, happiness. Out of disregard for life, love. Out of the attempt to crush the spirit, healing and nourishment. Maybe this is why I kept the book. It shares hard-learned skills of living beauty awake even in the most difficult of settings. Mandela's gardening was not the hobby of a retired person. Rather, it was a powerful, mindfulness training ground for one who would become a beacon of love, courage, and renewal.

"You must find your own garden." These are the words Mandela speaks to Stengel. These powerful words have never left me. While still working at the university, I had helped to establish an intensive summer program called The Canadian School of Peacebuilding. People come from around the world to teach and to learn about ways to be peace in the world. In 2014, we decided that we would begin a Mandela Peace Garden at Canadian Mennonite University. For me, this was a response to Mandela's instruction to find your own garden. Using Mandela's garden at Pollsmoor Prison as our model, we found an old oil drum, cut it in half, and filled it with soil. That year at the opening program of The Canadian School of Peacebuilding, we explained how oil drums could be seen as a symbol of war, harm, and hoarding. We told the peacebuilders we needed their help to transform the symbol into one of life, love, and sharing. Each peacebuilder helped plant the seeds to begin our Mandela Peace Garden.

While I look with fondness on those times, Mandela's call to find your own garden remains strong in my ears. I wonder, how do I practice Mandela gardening now? How might elephant dancers take on some form of Mandela gardening as a mindfulness training?

What are those practices away from the world, that can deeply nourish, heal, and renew us, even in difficult circumstances, for the living and loving we have yet to do?

To answer these questions, we need to realize the difference between a hobby and a Mandela Garden.

Hobbies are a kind of retreat from the world designed primarily to benefit the doer. Mandela Gardening may be something we do apart from the world but for the purpose of renewing us for service to benefit others.

At this point, I see my writing as a kind of Mandela Gardening. While others play games, I withdraw to write. If there are fruits to my writing, they are shared with the world. Writing quiets my mind. At times, when others see only catastrophe, I can touch the beauty of life. It is life-affirming and creative. It renews me and is part of serving others.

I challenge fellow elephant dancers to find your own Mandela Garden. It can be a powerful means of nourishment, healing, and renewal. Likely, your garden will not look like a garden or even like my writing. You need to find your own version. To demonstrate how radically different Mandela gardens can look, I share with you now another practice from my past.

When I was a young adult, I was offered the opportunity to run an organization designed to bring people of all ages and all abilities into the wild—usually by canoe, sometimes by dogsled. I jumped at the opportunity. The first group I called was L'Arche Communities in Winnipeg. I knew about L'Arche from the writings of Jean Vanier and Henri Nouwen. I read everything they wrote. L'Arche Communities are places where people with disabilities and people without visible disabilities live together in a loving, vulnerable community. I knew my staff and I needed to learn from L'Arche how to live and love well together. So we offered L'Arche the opportunity to come on a canoe trip with us. It was wonderful training in loving, living, and letting go. Each year, we did another trip with the L'Arche, which was often the highlight of our year. We were all renewed in the beauty of the wild. Those were sacred times, Mandela gardening times.

Elephant dancers, I encourage you to find your own garden. Provoke others to find their Mandela garden, by sharing about yours. If you wish you can sign up for my Elephant Dancers Facebook group at
 www.jaremsawatsky.com/facebook
where you can share your practices in elephant dancing including your experiments in Mandela gardening.

{ 29 }

Practicing Self-Compassion with Toni Bernhard

One day in Paris, Toni Bernhard got sick with what appeared to be an acute viral infection. She has never recovered. The many specialists she's consulted agree that she is sick but aren't sure what's wrong. The consensus is that the flu-like virus compromised her immune system in some way. For 22 years before she got sick, Toni was a law professor at the University of California, Davis. For six of those years, she was the law school's Dean of Students. For the past 15 years she has been mostly confined to her bed. The whole lifetime of my daughters, Toni has been sick.

Toni has been an inspiration to me. The first time she came onto my radar was about a year after I went on long-term disability. A number of friends had told me I should write about the journey, but for a year I was not interested. When I started to look around to see who was writing about living well with disease, I found Toni. She is the author of three inspiring books:

- *How to Be Sick: A Buddhist-Inspired Guide for the Chronically Ill and Their Caregivers*
- *How to Wake Up: A Buddhist-Inspired Guide to Navigating Joy and Sorrow*
- *How to Live Well with Chronic Pain and Illness: A Mindful Guide*

While there are many books filled with medical advice and many on supporting caregivers, I found few books that were written by people living well with disease. Finding Toni inspired me to write and share my own journey.

During the decade before she got sick, Toni studied and practiced Buddhist approaches to life. So she now has 25 years of experience with Buddhist practices. Spirit Rock Meditation Center has been instrumental in nourishing her. The 411-acre California retreat center has been a hub, bringing Buddhist ways to the Western world. Spirit Rock's 27 teachers include well-known Buddhist author Jack Kornfield. Among the amazing group of visiting teachers are Daniel J. Siegel, Sharon Salzberg, Tara Brach, and Rick Hanson. The center has hosted the Dalai Lama, Alice Walker, and Thich Nhat Hanh. Toni teaches through her books and by doing interviews.

Like me, she knows that a cure is not likely. Like me, she likes living and wants to do it in a compassionate and healing way. Like me, she must wrestle with how to live well through decades of chronic illness.

I knew I had much to learn from this teacher. So, out of the blue, I contacted her and asked if she would participate in a video interview. To my delight, and at no small cost to her health, she agreed.

Some teachers teach from a boat by the sea. Some from the stage. But Toni teaches from her bed. She told me, "I've received thousands of emails from people who have read my books. They say the hardest thing to do is to be compassionate toward themselves. They also say it is the one thing the books have helped them the most with."

This is a striking statement. People with chronic illness must face layers and layers of problems—financial, relational, medical, social. But amid all these waves of problems, learning self-compassion is the hardest! And learning self-compassion is possible!

"All of my books include chapters on self-compassion because to me it is the most important thing you can cultivate in life, whether you are sick or not," she said.

"I will tell a story about one of my Buddhist teachers. She was running late to get somewhere. She was in such a hurry that she knocked her drink over in her car. When that happened, she said to herself, 'You stupid, clumsy idiot. You knocked your drink over.' If I were in my car with my husband and he knocked his drink over, I would never say to him, 'You stupid, clumsy idiot, you knocked your drink over.'" Toni laughed, hardly able to get such an absurd sentence out of her mouth. Then she continued in a calmer voice, "But we say things like this to ourselves all the time."

I laughed because I understand what she is saying. I used to go into a panic when I lost my wallet. Now I just expect to lose it and am much more patient with myself. When my sister-in-law scratched both of our cars, it did not bother me. I know I will be the one damaging our cars in the future. If I want to be compassionate with myself about these things, I cannot be judgmental with others now.

Toni continued to unravel the meaning of the story. "My view, based on observation and hearing from other people, is that we judge ourselves negatively due to cultural conditioning and conditioning from those who raised us and were influential in our lives. If you had a parent who said, 'You knocked over your milk! You're so clumsy,' then you internalize that and think you are clumsy.

"When I talk about cultural conditioning, I'm talking about the kinds of ads on TV that make us feel inadequate. For the first five to six years of my illness, I blamed myself. Well, no wonder. You turn on the TV and all you see are ads: 'Join this gym and you will never get sick.' 'Eat this food and you'll be healthy forever.' So when we are struggling—either mentally or physically—we tend to blame ourselves.

"What is self-compassion? 'Compassion' has become a word—sort of like 'mindfulness'—that everyone talks about so much that it starts to lose its meaning. Compassion is nothing more than acknowledging that you are suffering, and then being kind to yourself about it instead of thinking that there is something wrong with you and blaming yourself. We face difficulties every day. It comes with being alive. Compassion simply asks you to be kind to yourself when the going gets rough."

Then she tilted her head back, thinking hard, and said, "I have yet to come up with a good reason not to be nice to yourself. Now, I know that is easy to say but I am fortunate because once I had that realization, I no longer found it hard to be nice to myself. In other words, when I mess up, I don't turn it on myself. I have friends and family who are hard on themselves all the time. But that doesn't help anyone or anything."

Some of the most profound things I have learned are simple truths that resonated with me because of who it was that said them. Hearing the philosopher and humanitarian Jean Vanier smile and say, "God loves you" resounds because he has accompanied many people with mental and physical disabilities on the roller-coaster path of becoming human. Thich Nhat Hanh saying, "Every day I walk in the kingdom of God. Watch me"—and then taking a step, smiling, resounds in me because this is the person who stepped on the battlefields of Vietnam to collect bodies while the war was still raging. This is the person who criticized his own faith tradition for being too male-centered, too focused on getting out of this world. Toni's words strike me in a bit the same way. The one who has been in bed for 15 years, not knowing if she will get better or not, says, "Self-compassion is the most important thing that we can cultivate in life." It is doubly striking, as Toni does not even believe in the self as an independent entity.

Self-compassion is not a cure to magically fix our suffering because many things in life cannot be changed. Rather, self-compassion is part of the healing path and it has the potential to free us from suffering *about* suffering.

Toni is not interested in self-compassion as an idea. It is the practice of daily self-compassion as a way to let go of mental suffering and increase well-being that interests her. I highly recommend her books for this reason: they offer concrete, everyday practices to live in a more healing way, whether you are sick or not.

In my video recording, Toni and I explore the first Noble Truth, the Buddha's teaching on impermanence, and how to face sadness. To get a free copy, sign up for my Readers Group

(www.jaremsawatsky.com/more-healing)
and I will send it your way.

{ 30 }

Last Words

O ne of the secrets to thriving at the art of elephant dancing is to structure each day so that
you practice the steps.

Currently, this is my way of moving through the day:

Morning Schedule
- Be in awe of another day of life
- Eat like a thin Buddha
- Mindful walking and falling with the dog, being kind-ish to others
- Mandela gardening for nourishment and healing

Afternoon Schedule
- Learn something new about life
- Do a little bit of housework, laughing
- Eat like a fat Buddha – celebrate with friends and family
- Love the people around you
- Nourishing sleep

My home office is a desk in my third-floor bedroom, which overlooks a park. On the wall beside my desk is a whiteboard on which I have drawn a large five-petal flower. Each petal is one of the five mindfulness trainings, and each is a section of this book:

- Reverence for Life (Part I)—How do we continue to value life, even in the midst of a terminal disease?
- True Happiness (Part II)—Which habits can we cultivate to bring joy to ourselves and those around us?
- True Love (Part III)—How do we protect and nurture those closest to us?
- Loving Speech and Deep Listening (Part IV)—How can words and silence be used for healing on this journey?
- Nourishment and Healing (Part V)—How do we avoid toxins and consume mindfully?

These have been the inspiration for the structure and spirit of this book. Depicting them as a flower reminds me that this work of learning to dance with elephants is a work of beauty. It is my hope that many of you will take up the art of dancing with elephants and surpass my beginner's understandings of these things. My explorations in the art of dancing with elephants are yet incomplete. There is much to learn and much to unlearn. While I forget many things, these basics remain: life, happiness, love, nourishment, and healing. The greatest of these is love.

There is a story about Jesus' disciple, John, which says that in his final years, when he would speak, he would say only one word: love, love, love. Similarly, two days before Gandhi was assassinated, he said: "If I am to die by the bullet of a mad man, I must do so smiling. There must be no anger within me. God must be in my heart and on my lips." It seems to me that we elephant dancers might be inspired and tested by the following: When I die, can I do so smiling. Can there be no anger within me? Can love be in my heart and on my lips?

If I am able, I will try to keep writing and sharing about a more healing way of facing life, disease, and death. But at some point, I will lose my words. It is my hope that my last word is love.

Get Free 5-Part Video & Audio Series

Thank you for reading *Dancing with Elephants*, Vol 1 How to Die Smiling Series. I hope that reading it was as valuable for you as writing it was for me. To say thank you, I'd like to offer you a free copy of Vol 2 of the series when you sign up for my Readers Group.

The 5-part series (over 3.5hrs) includes conversations with Jon Kabat-Zinn, Patch Adams, Lucy Kalanithi, John Paul Lederach, Toni Bernhard. You can get the video & audio series for free by signing up at http://www.jaremsawatsky.com/more-healing/.

Also by Jarem Sawatsky

HOW TO DIE SMILING SERIES
- ***Dancing with Elephants***, Vol 1
- ***A More Healing Way***, Vol 2 (get free, http://www.jaremsawatsky.com/more-healing/)
- ***Living the Beauty of Imperfection***, Vol 3 (Coming March 2018 – Available for preorder now!)
    - o   Amazon Stores: myBook.to/living_beauty
    - o   Kobo: http://bit.ly/2znfWFI
    - o   Barnes and Noble: http://bit.ly/2ixnfAK
    - o   Buy on Nook: http://bit.ly/2y3HZGT
- More coming soon!

OTHER NONFICTION

- ***Voices of Harmony and Dissent: How Peacebuilders are Transforming Their World*** (Co-Edited by Richard McCutcheon, Valerie Smith and Jarem Sawatsky)
- ***Peacebuilders' Toolbox: 52 Online Resources For Peace Work*** (Co-Authored with Wendy Kroeker and Valerie Smith)

- *The Ethic of Traditional Communities and the Spirit of Healing Justice: Studies from Hollow Water, the Iona Community, and Plum Village*

- *Justpeace Ethics: A Guide to Restorative Justice and Peacebuilding*

Please Leave a Review

Enjoy This Book? You Can Make a Big Difference

Reviews are the most powerful tools when it comes to getting attention for my books. The secret to getting my books noticed is:

A committed and loyal bunch of readers like you.

Honest reviews of my books help bring them to the attention of other readers.

If you enjoyed this book, I would be very grateful if you could spend just five minutes leaving a review on Amazon. It can be as short as you like, even one sentence.

To leave a review, use one of the links below.
- www.amazon.ca/Dancing-Elephants-Mindfulness-Training-Dementia/dp/0995324204/
- www.amazon.com/Dancing-Elephants-Mindfulness-Training-Dementia/dp/0995324204

- www.amazon.co.uk/Dancing-Elephants-Mindfulness-Training-Dementia/dp/0995324204/
- www.goodreads.com/book/show/34069635-dancing-with-elephants

Acknowledgements

For me writing is a labour of love and one form of the art of Mandela gardening. But a lot of work goes into making my writing polished and readable for others. This is work I cannot do on my own. So I want to acknowledge, with the deep gratitude, the community of awesome people who helped make this book more than a possibility.

My friends encouraged me to write/blog my experience of facing Huntington's disease. When I first stopped working, I thought this was a bad idea and did nothing for a year. Then I began to realize the wisdom in this suggestion and I started the blog Dancing With Elephants: A Beginners Guide to Losing Your Mind
(www.jaremsawatsky.com/dancing-blog).
That blog was a springboard for this book.

To the thousands who read my blogs and those in my awesome Readers Group—your interest fueled mine. Without your engagement, I may well not have completed this book. Thank you.

To the detailed, wise, and compassionate Valerie Smith, who served as my developmental editor, thank you for making this project flow and shine.

To the meticulous and generous Dawn Raffel, volunteer copy editor-I am deeply honored.

To my team of proofreaders: Kerry Callan, Irene Estabrooks, Mona Lacey, Nathan Reimer, Andrew Sawatsky, Beth Sawatsky, Jamie Burton, Hannah Sawatsky, Rhona Sawatsky, Craig Terlson. Thank you for letting people focus on the content of this book, rather than on my mistakes.

To the artistic and inspiring cover designer Carl at Extended Imagery, thank you for working so boldly on this project. To my sister-in-law Beth Sawatsky who patiently and creatively took the author photo.

To my articulate and brave advance team of readers, it is your generosity of spirit which enlivens this book.

To Rhona, Sara, and Koila, thank you for supporting me—in your many ways—so I could pursue my tunnel vision infused writing.

To my readers, you are the reason I wrote this book. Thank you for engaging and sharing.

Deep thanks and gratitude to each of you.

About the Author

Jarem Sawatsky, PhD, is internationally known for his work as a writer, teacher, and peacebuilder, working to bring an engaged mindfulness for those interested in wellness, resilience, and transformation. He is Professor Emeritus of Peace and Conflict Transformation Studies at Canadian Mennonite University and the author of numerous books and articles on healing justice, peacebuilding, and restorative justice. Since being diagnosed with Huntington's disease, he has been blogging at Dancing with Elephants, exploring how peacebuilding and

mindfulness insights might help those facing chronic illness, dementia, and aging
(www.jaremsawatsky.com/dancing-blog).
He lives in Winnipeg, Canada, with his wife, twin daughters, and a golden Labrador.

He can be contacted in the following ways:
    Website: www.jaremsawatsky.com
    Readers Group:
        www.jaremsawatsky.com/readers

Dedication

For Rhona, Koila, and Sara—I hope by learning the art of dancing with elephants I will also learn how to love you more fully. You are my joy.

Made in the USA
San Bernardino, CA
10 March 2018